HOME LIFE

one

Home Life

VOLUME ONE

Alice Thomas Ellis

The Akadine Press

1997

Home Life *One*

A COMMON READER EDITION published 1997
by The Akadine Press, Inc., by arrangement with the author.

Originally published 1986 by Gerald Duckworth & Co. Ltd. as *Home Life*.

The essays collected in this book appeared originally as columns in *The Spectator*.

A COMMON READER EDITION and fountain colophon are trademarks of
The Akadine Press, Inc.

ISBN 1-888173-10-6

For Someone

HOME LIFE

one

Open house

A strange man appeared in the garden yesterday, mouthing and gesticulating at the dining-room window while Someone was quietly eating his lunch and reading the paper.

'Are you expecting a person in a brown coat?' I asked.

'No,' he said; 'tell him to go away' – or words to that effect.

So I went to the laundry-room door and leaned out. 'Yers?' I enquired, very lady of the manor.

He said he'd been observing the house for some time, it appeared to be unoccupied, which was a pity as it had some potential, and did I know if it was for sale?

Now there are three cats, four adults, one teenager and a child actually resident in this house. Janet comes in every day, Maureen comes once a week to do the rough,

Letitia comes to din some French into the head of the teenager, and every single day each one of us is visited by at least one friend – in the case of the teenager it's more like fifteen as they're at the age where they travel about in hordes, settling in different places until the householder loses patience and slings them out. People come to lunch and dinner, the postman plods up twice daily, Eric delivers the papers each morning, men come to read the gas meter or cut off the electricity, artisans arrive to mend things, and on the rare occasions when no one else is about tinkers nip in to pinch anything left lying around. (We have never caught one, and I think they may keep fern seed in their shoes which makes you invisible.) The house will be full of people who have incautiously left their jackets with their wallets in the pockets, or their handbags on the kitchen bench, and tinkers slither in like weasels and are away again in a trice bearing money and credit cards and car-keys and house-keys. They don't bother with actual articles of clothing, and if they take a handbag they remove anything of value and throw it over somebody's garden wall where policemen can find it. There isn't a great deal of point in having an empty handbag returned. Apart from the loss of cash, the nuisance lies in all that ringing up of banks and shops and having the locks altered.

Once they stole a basketful of dirty laundry and

helped themselves to the contents of the freezer. They
were starting on the china when Someone heard them and
came down to intervene. One of the things they took from
the freezer was an unlabelled bag of pet food – processed
kangaroo, salmonella flavour I should think, and I do so
hope they ate it. (I told the police if they saw a sick-looking
tinker they should promptly arrest him.)

When, I asked myself, could this man have been
watching the house? Surely not in the evening when, the
young being what they are, every room in the place is left
blazing with light, disco music roars from the top floor,
the TV is twittering away to itself in the drawing-room
and I'm down here clashing dishes and listening to the
Archers on the wireless. Maybe he comes round at dead of
night, but even then Someone is frequently burning the
midnight oil and Cadders is either prowling the wall or
inside trying conclusions with the other cats. The house
is seldom what you could describe as really quiet. I asked
Janet what she thought and she said maybe it was because
we didn't have any curtains. I said indignantly that we
jolly well did – great big velvet ones – and she said
we didn't have *net* curtains. But nor do the neighbours.
When you get bored with the telly you can walk up and
down watching intimate domestic dramas being played
out through tasteful picture windows in through-plan

semi-basements. Admittedly no garden looks its best in January, but when we've gathered up the waste paper that blows in from the market and collected the chicken 'n' chips packets and VP wine bottles that the indigenous population disposes of over the wall it looks quite neat. I agree the exterior could do with a lick of paint, but newly-painted houses look misleadingly prosperous (once you've decorated the front you've got no money left) and invite professional burglars.

I expect you are wondering why I spoke to this potential buyer through the laundry-room door. There are six doors to this house if you count the french windows, but they are all burglar-proof, and if you lose the keys they are householder-proof too and you can't open them, so we all go in and out through the laundry. When he comes to see us, Jeff is always impressed by the quantities of clean shirts hanging on a rail over the boiler, but, as I've said, we cater for three cats, four adults, one teenager and one child and that leaves a lot of washing even when the tinkers have taken half of it.

Fire and water

The Regius Professor of Greek and his wife, Mary, are
coming to lunch, and the pipes have frozen. What's for
lunch? Bread-and-butter pudding, that's what. It would
have been onion soup and saunders* and salad and bread-
and-butter pudding, but you can't make onion soup when
the pipes are frozen any more than you can boil potatoes
or wash lettuce. Mary who is American by birth says the
level of efficiency in this country makes her eyes water
and I know what she means. There's an overall air of
despairing lassitude, rather like the feeling one has oneself
when faced with a form to fill in or a teenager to get out
of bed. The second plumber I rang (the first was engaged)

* Saunders: mashed potato layered with mince meat.

suggested wearily that I should just let the pipes thaw naturally.

We had trouble in the country too. When we lit the fire in the sitting-room we discovered that the extractor fan had ceased to function. There are three chimneys on that house, not a million miles from each other, and two of them work perfectly. The third not only does not work, it seems to have a capacity to exude more smoke than is commensurate with the quantity of fuel on the fire. We puzzled about how those who are known locally as 'the old people' managed. They certainly didn't have extractor fans and must have been utterly kippered, *unless* – and we think this is probably the case – they knew something we don't, and have taken the secret to the grave.

I went to the grave of our second son on his birthday. He is buried in the churchyard which lies across two fields and a stream from the house. In the summer I met one of the women from the village there, and I said no one had ever told me, and I hadn't known, that one would go on missing them so much for so long and so long, and she said her daughter had died in infancy over forty years before and she still mourned her. There are those who have seen it as their duty to convince me, for my own good, that the dead are well and truly dead and we shall never see them again, but I can't take that seriously.

I always feel remarkably cheerful in the churchyard and don't want to leave. One of these days I won't have to, since we have acquired the land from the grave to the wall, and there is plenty of room for the rest of us. Somebody I know nearly bought a house once because it was adjacent to a graveyard and when the time came the family would merely have to tip her over the wall. It is comforting to know where one is going to end up. Lends a sense of security.

Returning to the house I noted that the guns were out, banging away at the pheasants. Remembering a harrowing Victorian tale of a little maiden in a fur tippet who was shot by her father in mistake for a rabbit, I suggested to the daughter and her friend that should they find themselves in the vicinity of the hunters they must shout 'Hold your fire'. This obviously struck them as a good scheme, for the next thing I knew they were up the mountain piping this phrase and I had to rush out and haul them back.

For a few days there was a heavy frost and clear pink skies, and one morning the birds posed themselves in the hazel outside the parlour window as though for an illustration in the British Book of Birds. All manner of passerines perched in its branches looking heartbreakingly beautiful; then a robin added itself to the group and it was

too much. Ralph Vaughan Williams was once travelling
through the Alps with his wife, Ursula. The sun was setting
with a fiery glow behind the snow-capped peaks, the dark
conifers were gleaming ice-spangled – you know the sort
of thing – so she nudged him and told him to look out
of the window. After a moment, as he regarded this scene,
he remarked that it looked like the watercolours in an
organist's drawing-room and turned back to his dinner.
Still, one mustn't get too refined. Taken to the limit, this
attitude would mean that one could only appreciate, say, a
view of the backside of Milton Keynes from the motorway
on a mid morning in February.

One day, feeling a bit frail, what with the fumes and
the pipes and the measures I had taken to calm myself,
I lay on the sofa and watched telly in the afternoon,
which I think is something on a par with eating chocolates
before breakfast. Well, serves me right. I saw an old film
which must surely be the most frightful ever made. It was
entitled *Sentimental Journey* and featured a woman who kept
calling people 'dear': a very threatening appellation which
always causes me to look for cover when thus addressed.
Undeterred even by death, she kept coming back in the
sharp satin robe she was wearing when she snuffed it, to
harass the moppet who also ran by telling her she must
look after the hero, a fully-grown male, because he was so

little. To whoever conceived that film I would say I don't claim to know what the dead are doing, but I bet they're not doing that – dear.

P.S. The daughter has just come home because the pipes in her school have frozen.

Fur flying

A friend whom I hadn't seen since the summer popped in the other day sporting a new moustache, and I said 'Good heavens, what have you got on your face?' Which was rude. He riposted by implying that my earrings were showy, and after that we got on with our usual amity. It has been a week of personal remarks. One morning I came flying downstairs in hot pursuit of the cat Cadders before I had pinned up my hair, and Janet, gazing at me thoughtfully, remarked with admirable candour, 'You look very common with your hair down.' I bought a new frock to restore my confidence but have decided it makes me look like Carrie Pooter, or possibly Ethel le Neve before she got into cross-dressing. It is all gathered in at the waist which is dropped to just below the knee. My daughter despises it, so at least it will be all my own.

Having had only sons until she turned up, I had not understood what the mothers of daughters suffer. The boys used to pinch my henna and hair spray, but they left my clothes alone (except for briefly borrowing my jodhpurs – I think because the things are thirty years old and have a rakish, indefinable but definite military air about them). Daughters, who now seem to grow as large as their mothers before they even reach puberty, are a menace, knowing instinctively which shoes you are planning to wear that day and getting in first. My mother was the youngest of seven sisters and in her house it was known as 'First up, best dressed!'. I bought a pair of gents' pyjamas for Someone at the same time as my frock. Real ones with stripes and pockets and none of that paisley nonsense. There was a note attached to one of the buttons in English, French, Italian and German. The French, roughly translated, says they were Fabricated Soigneusely from Noble Tissues for the Exigent Man of Today. The English says they were Carefully Manufactured from Fine Fabrics for your Ultimate Comfort. The recipient said he'd expect to find that assurance on his shroud, but I got very suspicious and pulled them this way and that to see if they were likely to fall to pieces at the first wash. It's like those notices you see outside pubs saying 'Good Food'. I always take this as a warning that the food is probably stinking awful, because otherwise why bluster about it.

My mother used to tell me that if I persisted in reading *The Girl's Crystal* under the bedclothes with a torch after lights-out I would undoubtedly lose the sight of my eyes and I'm beginning to wonder if she was right. I keep assaulting my handbag, which I habitually leave on the kitchen table, under the impression that it is the cat, Cadders. They are much the same size and shape and exactly the same colour. Cadders steals meat and cheese and cream and custard. He tears open the bin liners to eat the herring bones. Then he comes in to be sick. He has broken the chimney of an oil lamp, a key-patterned sherry glass, several wine glasses and one of a pair of jugs. He chases our original cat, a charming creature known simply as Puss, all over the house until she ends up leaping from shelf to shelf in the china pantry, through the Asiatic Pheasant dish-covers, to cower in an alcove. He has also ruined her disposition. Unable to retaliate against him because he is a great big brute, she has taken to beating up the many-toed or arboreal cat, who is not only smaller than her but may well be expecting. For a time we tried putting him out at night. His owner (who seems to have moved away from home again) says he is a nocturnal beast, but when he isn't waging war with the neighbouring mogs on the kitchen roof he is hammering to be let in. I have told his owner he will have to take a room in a hotel for either me or Cadders. I don't care which.

The other night the bath plug was missing. For a theft so inexplicable no solution is too bizarre, and I immediately suspected Russians, since I don't think even that cat would nick the bath plug.

These domestic mysteries are most irritating. Why, for instance, is the rug in one of the bedrooms covered in rice and chickpeas? Why is the handle of a plastic hairbrush sticking out of a broken pane in the glasshouse, and what happened to the wooden-backed hairbrushes? Whose is the jacket and set of keys in the boiler-room, and how is he managing without them? How did we once accumulate eighty odd socks, and where do the teaspoons go? What is the greenish culture on a plate at the back of a bookshelf, and who rings up and doesn't say anything and why don't I care? Where is the pink-rimmed trifle dish, and where was J. Bernard last Tuesday lunchtime? I know where his lunch was. It was here, coated in oatmeal and fried to a turn. Someone else had it for his tea. Then I wrapped up its bones in newspaper and a plastic bag and put them in the bin-liner and Cadders got them out again . . .

But, there, I mustn't let myself be driven to paranoia by a cat.

.

Drink up

Someone has given me an interesting book about women and alcoholism. Thank you, darling. We answered the questionnaire which it contains and my score indicated that I was harming myself and possibly causing suffering to others. Well, I feel all right and it's some time since I attacked anyone in a drunken fury or threw up on their carpet, and I don't leave the kiddies shivering outside the pub, so don't feel too guilty. It goes on to warn that I will experience unpleasant withdrawal symptoms if I try to give up. I am often forced to give up in the country since the off-licence is miles away, and I don't drive (in these circs if you don't drive you can't drink) and I usually experience nothing more than mild annoyance.

Though I must confess that once, in the country, with

a houseful of little boys and no help, I decided that I would go mad without something to take the edges off everything, and I walked into Bala, or rather slithered, since the snow was thick on the ground, and I took the baby in a basket on a sledge. The distance both ways amounted to nearly twelve miles, so there's dedication for you. I felt wonderful as I made it back just before nightfall.

On the other hand I once took a child to see a doctor about a verucca. The doctor was bored stiff with the verucca. He looked keenly at me, enquired what was wrong and on hearing that I had sustained a bereavement pressed upon me an unsolicited prescription. Being half-witted, I cashed it in and started on a course of pills which had to be approached warily – one a day for two days, two a day for three days – that sort of thing. After a week of this I found I could no longer read newsprint, my mouth was as dry as a dog biscuit and every time I stood up I fell over. Vodka never did that to me.

Nothing does anything much for grief, but just a little alcohol helps just a little, especially at funerals. A wake would not be the same with everyone standing round, carefully timing his anti-depressants. My friend Alfred, when he was a little lad, went to an Irish wake, got a touch drunk and offered a glass to the person propped up in bed, only to discover that it was the corpse. It gave him a bit of a turn, but then he reasoned that it was fair enough that the principal should be present. It was *his* funeral after all.

Still, I admit that many of us do drink too much. I was once sitting with some people when it was announced that an actress had died of a drink-related disease. She had drunk half a bottle of brandy a day. There was an appalled silence, broken at last by somebody who whispered, 'But that's what we *all* drink, every day after dinner, when we've drunk everything else.'

Someone says women and children don't need to drink because they're drunk already. I don't know quite what he means by this, but agree that children should abstain. People under 18 are unable to make it to the lavatory before they are overwhelmed by nausea. A young visitor was once sick in the telephone. They have incapacitating hangovers and demand bed rest, and they often drink things which the adults had put aside for themselves. The more unscrupulous then fill up the bottles with water. It is embarrassing to find you have poured a guest a measure of Adam's ale from a Smirnoff bottle.

One way of giving up drinking is to stop going to parties. Going to parties and sipping bitter lemon is no good. Watching everyone else getting merry, confidential, abusive, speechless or whichever way it takes them is at once highly revealing and intensely boring. I have worked out a method of not going to parties which causes no offence. You accept the invitation and when the evening comes you wash your hair, go to bed early with a good book and wake refreshed and wholesome in the morning. Then you write a thankyou letter on the following lines – 'Darling, a wonderful party. I was sorry to slip away without saying goodbye, but you were getting on so well with that good-looking blonde (or whatever, according to your host's/hostess's predilections) that I felt reluctant to intrude.' If you should *wish* to be offensive you can add an exclamation mark. The tone of the note depends on what you know of the person who hoped to entertain you. If you don't like him much you could say 'I do hope you're feeling a little better today,' and if you really hate him you could say, 'I don't expect an apology but I feel we would be wise not to meet for some time.' It only works for fairly large parties. I think even the most bibulous of hosts would smell a rat if the occasion had been a dinner party for two.

School report

Our youngest child recently started at the local Comprehensive over the way but has refused to attend for the past few days for fear of being beaten up. It seems there are two factions there, known by their attire as the Trendies and the Casuals, between whom there is enmity. Oh, well, you say, boys will be boys. Yes, but these are *girls*. I don't know what Miss Buss and Miss Beale, the founders, would make of it. I never felt at ease in school uniform, but at least it required no thought and there was no argument. One clambered each morning into bloomers, gymslip and the terrible hat, and there you were. I get weary now with the daily discussions as to the relative merits of the sensible dark sweater and the T-shirt, emblazoned with the legend 'Funny Farm. Out for the day'. Please, *why* did they do away with school uniform? And how do we persuade an adamant eleven-year-old that it's worth running the risk of getting socked to go and be educated?

Another local school displays a notice reading, 'Keep Out. Security Guards and Dogs Patrolling School Grounds and Buildings'. This occasions ironic smiles in a number of parents who see the problem primarily as one of keeping the kiddies *in*. We've been through it all before. Our third son, after his first day at school, imagined that that was all. He'd been told he was going to school, he'd been to school, and now he expected his life to resume the even tenor of its ways.

Then our fourth son went briefly to an establishment where he was required to play rugger. After the first game he announced that he had walked on to the field, fifteen bloody big blokes had dropped on top of him and he wasn't going any more. Later he joined the Territorial Army, and now his chief recreation is jumping out of aeroplanes, so one can draw no significant conclusions as to a person's courage from these early responses. I can't even count the number of words on this page with any degree of accuracy, and I can't remember what the geography mistress told me about Bogota, although I know she told me something. My favourite thing at that time was playing in the granite quarry when the quarrymen had gone home and I resented time wasted on homework. I also resented walking a mile downhill to the station in a blinding gale and a mile uphill at the other end. It was much pleasanter to stay by the kitchen range with a bag of humbugs and the *Beano*.

I have to admit that I found skool pretty good hell. People fall into two categories – those who enjoyed their school days and those who didn't, and all the people I like best fall into the latter category. There has to be something peculiar about anyone who liked school.

When we started on the dreary round we discovered very soon that if you approach a State school with a view to entrusting a child to its care and you learn that what it really prides itself on is its orchestra then you can confidently expect the majority of its charges eventually to leave with a certificate – CSE, failed. This awareness has saved us from suffering too many school concerts. In my view a child with a musical instrument is to be avoided at all costs, and a number of children forming a chamber group should be told to stop it at once. Next in horror to the school concert is the Open Evening which necessitates standing in line behind some fathead who is determined to follow through with every single teacher every single aspect of his offspring's scholastic achievement, social adjustment, psychiatric balance, allergic responses, dietary requirements, etc etc, if it takes him all night. As it often does. Sometimes, eavesdropping on the close-questioning, you wonder whether the parent has actually met the child, so avid is he for detailed information.

But possibly the worst experience of all is being summoned to the Head's study. The purpose of the interview is seldom conducive to one's peace of mind; rarely stemming from an impulse on the part of the Head to assure you that your child is an ornament to the school. Even when the object of the meeting is simply to discuss O level options I feel uncomfortable and keep glancing wistfully out of the window at the other children (at these times one regresses to the age of about eight) running round in the fresh air, carefree and unconcerned. Sometimes, though not often, one finds oneself at cross-purposes with Teacher because he seems to be referring to a child unknown to one: a helpful, courteous, hard-working, retiring child who eats up all his greens. As a friend of mine once remarked — can we be speaking of the *same* Tarquin B. Hasselburger? Red hair and freckles? Form C?

Labour of love

People have started getting married again. We all did it at one time, but then it seemed to go out of fashion. Now my acquaintance is divided fairly evenly between those who are desperate to get married and those who are equally desperate to get divorced. I have myself been in love for ages with Captain Brown in *Cranford*. He reminds me of our next-door neighbour who unfroze the pipes for us with a hairdryer. Another neighbour remarked that now I would know what to do next time, and I said 'Yes, go screaming round to Robin.' I am very fond of handsome, helpful men. That may sound self-evident but I know a lot of women who actually *prefer* fat ugly little bastards.

It is impossible for the dispassionate observer to understand what people see in each other. Sometimes

I have sniffled unreservedly at weddings but just as often I have stared at the backs of the bridal couple standing before the altar and wondered what on earth they were doing there. I think it was Kingsley Amis who was struck by much the same thought on seeing some ladies waiting outside a nursery school: how did they get to be mummies? Love is not merely blind but mentally afflicted and I suppose we should all be grateful, though when I think of the tears that have, over the years, soaked into my shoulder from people of all sexual persuasions wailing for a lost love who was, in my view, a perfect horror, I begin to wonder again.

It is no use reminding the abandoned one that the beloved was a monster. This only leads to fresh tears and cries of 'I know, but I loved him/her so!'. Nor is it any use to insist that men have died and worms have eaten them but not for love. The newly bereft cannot believe it. Frequently, of course, while everyone is still creeping round with comforting mugs of Ovaltine and speaking in hushed tones the sorrowing one comes bouncing in with a brand new monster and this is, regrettably, less gratifying than irritating.

Still, a wedding is always a good excuse to buy new clothes. Janet and I have noticed over the years that the upper classes go to weddings in clothes that are already

hanging in their wardrobes and even the men need no
recourse to Moss Bros. She and I, daughters of the people,
shoot off down the West End or start poring over pattern
books. We get a lot of simple fun in church trying to work
out who's who from their apparel. Last time the totally
inexplicable lady in the crimplene dress, the fur stole and
the pudding-bowl hat turned out to be the vicar's wife.
We were very relieved to discover this, since otherwise
we would still be speculating. Then the wedding present
always poses a problem. There are some people who have,
as it were, a gift for presents. B. Bainbridge has a genius for
it. I have not. My imagination runs out at socks for men,
soap for ladies, rattles for babies and toasters for weddings.
Sometimes if I do think of something nice I have an
unworthy and cynical urge to specify on the accompanying
note that when the divorce occurs my present is to go with
the party of whom I am most fond. It is maddening to
think of the faithless monster gloating over one's stilton
dish.

Queen Victoria didn't like weddings, considering that
they had an indelicate flavour. I think she was right. I
always get prickly heat listening to the speeches veering
uneasily between pious hopes that Bob and Bets will
spend many years together in Christian wedlock and jests
about nighties. All a bit misplaced these days anyway,

since the happy couple have usually been shacked up together for ever and have only decided on marriage to confound the tax man. One thing I have noticed is that, contrary to popular belief, the bride is usually in a terrible twitter and much more nervous than the groom. I have also been forced to concede, again flying in the face of popular opinion, that on the whole men make less fuss when ill than women. Someone I know disbelieves in the germ theory of disease, resolutely refuses to admit that he could be anything so epicene as ill and, as a consequence, seldom is. He is also very brave when he cuts himself, running cold water over the wound and demanding that people should stop fussing. I insist on a lot of fuss if I have so much as a hangnail. I had to lie down for days recently when I damaged my toe. I had been almost overwhelmed by an urge to kick Someone but had thought I'd better not, so I'd kicked the sofa instead. Unfortunately I missed the soft bit and kicked the frame and crippled myself.

A final word on love. Somebody has sprayed a message on a sheet of metal on a bridge which reads 'Bruce loves Ruby', and underneath somebody else, presumably Bruce, has written: 'Oh no he doesn't'.

Power of speech

I have an early work by Mrs Beeton which she wrote for the 'smaller establishment': that is, a household with only a cook, a couple of maids and a boy to carry the coal. She says firmly, 'On entering the kitchen invariably say "Good morning Cook".' OK, you ponder, but what if Cook is out on the area steps dallying briefly with the muffin man? What if your household is so small you don't *have* a cook? Still, many housewives talk to themselves. I often say things aloud when I spill the milk or trip over the cat and there's no one here to listen. I plod round M&S muttering 'prawns, butter, underpants' because otherwise I forget what I'm doing there, and so do a lot of other ladies. One has to keep talking or one loses the knack. When the children were very small I spent weeks alone with them high up in the Welsh hills and I used to lose the power of speech. I would return to London bereft of all vocabulary, communicating in grunts and diddums talk. You feel a fool asking, for instance, Professor Sir Alfred Ayer if he would care for an icky bitty more soup in his ickle bowl.

But conversation can be dangerous, especially boring conversation which may have the effect of making one hysterical. I know a girl who was once visited by an old friend of her mother's, up from the country for the day. They went through the subjects of the canker in Bonzo's ear, the success of Mummy's calceolarias in the Flower Show, the state of Daddy's handicap and the cold in the vicar's nose, and then the visitor enquired, 'Now, how are you, dear? What have *you* been doing?' And my friend who had done nothing but wash nappies, trundle the baby round the shops and hoover the carpet suddenly went mad. She began, 'Oh, nothing much . . .' then she said, 'No, I tell a lie. I committed adultery last Wednesday afternoon.'

Of course other people's conversations often sound more interesting than the one you are currently engaged in, especially in restaurants. I have frequently lost the thread of what somebody was saying to me in trying to eavesdrop on the fascinating chat two tables away.

'Shut up,' I hiss. 'I'm trying to listen.' Very rude, but other people have such engrossing love lives. I am speaking here of women. Men in conversation together are dreadfully boring. They talk about money and work and the games they've been playing. Janet once came back late from shopping because she was absolutely rivetted by a conversation of unparalleled bawdiness between two ladies in Boots. She followed them round all the shelves peering at bottles of shampoo and idly fingering the tins of cat food, longing to ask them to speak up.

There are some people with whom it is extremely difficult to converse at all. You sit over the luncheon table and your guest chews placidly away at his lemon sole, not uttering a squeak. So you raise a topic; he deals with it succinctly and sticks a bit of bread and butter in his mouth. You raise another topic; he wipes the floor with it and takes a sip of Soave. At the end of the meal you feel as though you'd been running round the block for a day and a half. Unless you've been married to him for nearly thirty years it is hopelessly unnatural to sit over a meal with someone in silence. The person to whom I have been married for nearly thirty years was recently playing tennis, as is his wont, and I was sitting in the bar toying with a pint of bitter and being entertained by the club bore who suddenly remarked 'I like your husband so much that I am going to pay him the enormous compliment of not seducing you.' As they say, there's no answer to that one. A real conversation stopper. The next most maddening thing I ever heard was said to me only the other day by a friend who remarked affectionately that I was a terrible woman and went on to add that I was a clever old thing. Now I don't at all mind being called a terrible woman but I cannot begin to describe to you how decisively I draw the line at being called a clever old thing.

Very occasionally one does come out with the perfect response at the time instead of at three o'clock the following morning. Many years ago we knew a girl who called herself a friend. She was so sweet that if you bit her you'd damage your teeth. One day we were sitting chatting and Someone said that he would shortly be going to Paris on a business trip. 'Ooh,' she lisped, 'I love Parith. Thall I come with you?' Then she turned to me and said, 'Oh but you wouldn't like that, would you darling?' And quick as a flash I said, 'Well, I wouldn't mind in the least, darling, but *he* would *hate* it.'

Sometimes when I'm sad I remember that moment and it cheers me up no end.

Spectral

The many-toed or arboreal cat is on heat again. Each evening there are frightful screams from the garden and we rush out to rescue her from her suitors but she does not thank us. My friend Virginia once lived twelve floors up in a New York apartment building with umpteen doors, and doormen on guard. She had a female cat who was never permitted to go out into the dangers of the city; nevertheless this cat, several times, contrived to have a litter of kittens which, given the circumstances, you would think, was impossible. I suggested to Virginia that she should tell the Bishop of Durham but she said she couldn't be bothered. Leafing through my little black book I came across the heading 'Ghosts' and under it is listed the Archdeacon of Durham because, I hasten to explain,

I once read a newspaper article which indicated that he is prepared to believe in them. I find this interesting in view of the fact that the Bishop appears not to believe in anything, and I have a fantasy image of the pair of them sitting over sherry in the Close. Enter a spectre, clanking:

Spectre: 'Wheeee.'
Archdeacon: 'Good heavens, a ghost.'
Bishop (removing sherry from his reach): 'Nonsense, Archdeacon.'

I always feel cheated because I have never actually *seen* a wraith and am one of the few people I know who is fervently sure of their existence – and of flying saucers and the Loch Ness Monster and Spring Heel Jack and Herne the Hunter, and quite possibly the Telwyth Teg.

Once in Wales we used to hear, very clearly, the inexplicable sound of a hammer striking an anvil. This was in broad daylight and we would race round the barns hoping to find, perhaps, a closet blacksmith, but there was never anyone there. We weren't frightened since some parts of Wales are magical and some are holy and this was one of the holy places. (There *are* exceptions of course. Rhyl, for instance, is neither.) The third son and a number of his friends, sleeping out one year, swore that they had heard the sound of the laughter of women, but I put that down to the Pils. Then last summer we had the *breathing*. There was a friend staying, who is among other things a moth-watcher (to do this you wait till nightfall, hang a white sheet over the washing line, shine a lantern on it and sit back).

One night he came in looking a bit peculiar and said that there was a noise out there. We asked what sort of noise and he said it was someone breathing. Two of the boys, prudently taking an air rifle and the poker, went out to listen and when they came back they too said there was something breathing. This is the moment when everyone else struggles up crossly from his armchair and goes outside with the intention of saying 'Nonsense'. We started to do this and then were surprised to find that we were forced to agree. The breathing was loud and regular and steady like that of somebody sleeping. Everyone began to make characteristic diagnoses. Janet inferred it was a squirrel akip up a tree. The daughter said it was the puma, who is regularly sighted all over the country. I said it sounded to me as though a drunk had dropped off in a ditch. We drifted round speculating thus fruitlessly and eventually went to bed. All this time the tenor of the breathing changed not one jot. The next night some people came to dinner and when it grew dark I suggested that we should go out and listen, not really imagining that there would be anything to hear, but there it was: regular breathing, even louder than the previous night. There were ten of us altogether and we fanned out, the more agile and adventurous scrambling up the hillside and the rest of us looking round the hazel bushes and searching under the damson tree. As fast as one of us yelled that it was getting louder down here, somebody up the hill would screech back that it was getting louder up there. We were scratching round for hours, and again the tenor of the breathing changed not one jot. Among the witnesses present were my friend Celia who is the village sub-postmistress, and Linda Mary who is a Church of England chaplain.

The next night the sound had gone and I rather missed it. I asked Linda Mary what she thought had happened and she told me coolly that she had exorcised it. Without so much as a by-your-leave. I was rather annoyed, having felt proprietorial about it, but in the end I had to concede that she was probably right. As she explained, if it was an unquiet spirit it would be better off with the Lord.

They could have done with Linda Mary on the set of *The Shining*. She would have saved them an amazing amount of trouble.

Bailiffs

A very cheeky letter from the bailiffs proposing to imprison Someone, or maybe me. It begins with a fine impartiality – Dear Sir/Madam, Re: Rate Arrears. The thing is that when they dunned us they didn't dun us for enough, so it's their silly fault. It all started when Someone discovered yet another person in the garden peering through the windows. He asked what he was doing and the man said he was a bailiff, showed him a sheet of paper describing the contents of the house – washing machine, tumble dryer and a lot of tatty old books and went on to speak of something quite incomprehensible called 'walking distraints' or something. Someone said he was sorry to put him to all that trouble and the man said,

Not to worry, if it wasn't for people like us he'd be out of a job.

I have quite often heard people say that they wouldn't mind a spell in the slammer – no responsibilities and a chance to catch up on *Swann's Way*, and write the autobiography they'd always intended, but those with first-hand experience never seem at all keen on it. Except for one lady I met some time ago who used to go round in black leather, a series of chains and a crash helmet. She would punctuate her conversation with the remark, 'Of course, you realise I'm a lesbian.' To which people would respond, 'Cor, you never are. Fancy that.' She used to demonstrate about things, and she liked going to Holloway because there were so many girls there.

I once visited a friend in one of the more modern penal establishments and apart from a great deal of conspicuous locking and unlocking of doors it was rather like being in the motorway caff – a lot of formica and glass and an overall feeling that on the whole you'd rather be somewhere else. It's the same with nervous breakdowns. People who have never had one seem to imagine it would offer the opportunity for a nice rest, forgetting that sensations of nameless terror and total personal inadequacy are not very conducive to peace of mind.

On the other hand, I'm hooked on Beaumaris jail, in Wales, which is now unoccupied. It reminds me of the National school where I went as an infant, and was built at much the same date. They both have an air of solid assurance, and even the jail has a heavily respectable feeling about it. The female felons used to work in the laundry while the men were busy on the treadmill round the back, and though it was clearly no rest home I have sometimes thought I might not have desperately resented being incarcerated there: except for the diet, which was boring in the extreme – bread, gruel and a weekly bowl of gristle – though it probably compared well enough with what the average servant would have received at the time. The cells have little windows and primitive washbasins and, provided one didn't have to share, they are preferable to most motel bedrooms. I could have taught a little mouse to love me, or possibly a nice clean rat – the bright-eyed sort who sit up and wash their whiskers, not the kind who live in sewers and chew people's extremities while they sleep. Jailers in stories always have daughters to be kind to the prisoners, and I wonder whether they ever have sons to look after the interests of lady criminals. It seems doubtful. I think Lord Longford has taken that role on himself, although I know there are many other people who visit prisoners too. I hope they're all amusing. I discovered in hospital that a lot of people who can't get anyone else to listen to them had a wonderful time boring the pants off patients who are frequently shackled to their beds by traction and in no position to make their excuses and hop it. Prison must be worse.

The only really creepy, nightmare-inducing part of Beaumaris jail is the death cell, which contains a harrowing account of a condemned murderer who took such a dim view of the whole business that he resolutely refused to be so accommodating as to permit himself to be hanged without protest, barricading himself in his cell with his bench, refusing to listen to reason and closing his ears to the chaplain, governor and hangman who were grouped outside, imploring him to come out and be killed like a gent. He said he hadn't done it. When they finally winkled him out and dragged him to the scaffold he said that on the instant of his death the clock opposite the jail would stop and would never go again. And it did and it hasn't – though it has to be admitted that most of the clocks in public places throughout the country seem to be suffering from the same syndrome for whatever reason. When I was a little girl they all worked. My mother describes it bitterly as 'progress'. When I was the age the daughter is now, slaving away in my National school, I used to get my sums wrong on a slate using a slate pencil. Now I get them wrong on the kiddies' calculators. Which reminds me that I should apply myself to the word-processor and sort out this little matter of the bailiffs. Otherwise I shall end up inside.

Salt 'n blood

It is not generally acknowledged how very contentious is
the subject of food and cookery. I lost my temper recently
because one of my dearest friends made himself a little
snack half an hour before dinner. It wasn't the timing that
made me so cross, although that was sufficiently annoying:
it was the nature of the snack. This is what he did. He took
a slice of bread, placed upon it two raw rashers of bacon
and two slices of raw apple, and then covered it with
chopped cheese. I watched incredulously as he put it in
the oven. 'The bacon won't cook,' I said. 'The apple will
half cook, the bread will burn and the cheese will frizzle,
but the bacon will merely get warm!' He said tranquilly
that it would be delicious, and sat down to wait while I
wondered whether to throw myself on the floor and drum

my heels. Later as I prepared a chicken curry he suggested that I should put bananas in the sauce and I cracked again. 'You don't put bananas in the sauce, you terrible fool,' I snarled. 'If you have bananas with it at all you serve them raw, sliced and sprinkled with a little lemon juice.' He said he couldn't see the difference. He also eats toast and marmalade at the same time as his boiled egg (no salt). Mouthful of marmalade, mouthful of egg. Ugh.

I don't know why this is so enraging, but I get the same feeling in those restaurants which have taken to serving stuff like noisettes of lamb coated in chopped anchovy and garnished with peach purée. 'Why?' I whine querulously. 'Why have they done that? Why not strawberry conserve with turbot?' The prospect of turnip and rhubarb soup fills me with gloom, and I hate the sight of slices of kiwi fruit. Down-market it's mandarin oranges. I once read in a women's mag a recipe for baked potatoes stuffed with smoked mackerel and topped with mandarin orange slices. But then you can't really blame the women's mags, because once they've decided to run a cookery column they have to find new things to put in it and it must be amazingly difficult. I couldn't do it. All I can remember most days is shepherd's pie, and bangers and mash, and something roasted on Sunday. While there is obviously a place for imagination in the kitchen, I sometimes get the impression that the chef has gone mad. Gazing wild-eyed at a boring old chicken, he thinks: 'Let us marinade it in pina colada and top it off with a helping of salt cod and half a walnut.' I took Janet out to lunch a while ago for a special treat. She had a veal chop which was flanked by a solitary langoustine looking exactly like something that had fallen off its horse, and this too was astonishingly, disproportionately, irritating. What was it *doing* there? I blame the Belgians. Soon after the war we went to Lier on holiday and to this day I remember a bowl of cherries with meat balls in it, and last summer in Bruges we had beef casserole with stewed apricots. Or maybe it's *Just William* – sardine and raspberry jam sandwiches.

Still, while restaurants can be exasperating, the most dangerously inflammatory place is one's own kitchen. My hackles rise if I see people who have offered to help cutting up onions the wrong way or peeling potatoes thickly with a knife instead of thinly with a peeler or throwing away half the lettuce. After nearly ten years I still have a compulsion to remind Janet to rinse the deleterious steel filings off the carving-knife after sharpening it, and not to put salt in the stew before the meat is tender. She takes it quite well, merely throwing me a warning glance, and I freely concede that she makes better french dressing than me (I can never be bothered with the pinch of mustard which helps it emulsify) and better pastry. In the days when there were a lot of them about, cooks were notorious for murdering and being murdered, and I do see why. Picture the scene: cook in a blazing hot kitchen, slightly stunned on cooking sherry, venison going soot-black on the new mechanical spit, Spotted Dick boiling dry, oysters beginning to whiff a bit, the smoke pouring down the chimney as the wind changes, and the boning knife freshly honed on the kitchen table. Enter another member of the household. This injudicious person strolls across to where the cornflour sauce is sullenly bubbling on the range, idly sticks in a finger, licks it and remarks: 'I say, Cook, this tastes remarkably like paper-hanger's paste.' What happens next is best performed off stage, so we'll leave it there.

P.S. I learn that the veal/langoustine wheeze is a pale imitation of an American vulgarism called Surf 'n' Turf, best bit of fillet steak served with half a lobster. The thinking behind this is similar to that which leads some potentates to force feed their women until they have to be rolled around. Conspicuous consumerism, I believe it's called.

Nicked

One of our neighbours was burgled again the other day. People who have been burgled once always seem to be burgled again. One of my friends grew rather offended when on three occasions thieves scorned to take the candelabra from her dining-room table. She began to wonder what the professional eye could see that she couldn't. The neighbour's burglars arrived at teatime when he was sitting quietly in his study and his little girl was playing the piano in the basement and eating marmite sandwiches. The King Charles spaniel, Ben, went woof, woof, or rather, as my neighbour supposed, wolf, wolf, since he's always doing it, but then he heard footsteps in the room above and going up to investigate he noticed a colossal policeman attempting to kick in the back door, screaming, 'Let me in, he's getting away.' Somewhat bemused, the neighbour complied and there followed a very thrilling few moments. The neighbourhood children spent a blissful evening when the Criminal Investigation Department arrived with a case full of fingerprint powder, the daughter resolutely refusing to come home for her French lesson. It was just as though the cast of a TV Cops and Robbers had emerged from the set for their personal delectation. The robbers in question got away but not before one of them had left what is delicately known as his 'calling card' on the bedroom carpet. I can never understand this particular manifestation of criminal behaviour because you'd think if you had a quick get-away in mind the last place you'd want your trousers to be was round your ankles. The neighbour saved it as evidence but the police said people always did that and what were they supposed to learn from it, and the neighbour said the burglar's last meal had clearly consisted of sweetcorn if that was any help. Goodness how disgusting.

Many years ago I caught a burglar. He was only seven and when I collared him he burst into tears, so I wiped his nose and gave him a marmite sandwich, and ever since then he's been one of the family, working in the office, standing godfather to the daughter and bringing the house back into shape when it gets right out of control. Fate plays some funny tricks, since not only is he one of the most efficient people I've ever known but he makes me laugh, and I don't quite see what we'd have done without him. He and his Mum recently moved into a new flat with the dog who is called Sally. They met the lady next door who is also called Sally and who kindly offered to take Alfred to show him the best places to shop. He took the dog too and every so often he said, 'Sit, Sally, you silly bitch!' and things like that, which led to a great deal of misunderstanding until he realised the confusion of nomenclature and explained.

He was here one day looking out of the window at the rain when a girl shot in through the gate and crouched down between the hortensia and the dustbin. 'There's a girl out there with a bag full of jewels,' he observed nonchalantly. As he spoke, two men tore past, looking to right and left. I don't know why but in cases like this one's instincts seem to run in favour of the fugitive. It was pouring with rain; she was shaking like a jelly; so we brought her in, gave her a marmite sandwich and put her a few questions. It transpired that she and two friends (both men) had just relieved a local furniture shop of some crystal chandeliers, which explained the jewels. They had been apprehended by the shop assistants and the men had fled leaving her to carry the can, or rather the swag.

We said, Tsk tsk, that was very naughty, wasn't it, and she must promise never to do it again, but we'd overlook it this time – which was pretty reprehensible, I suppose, since they weren't *our* crystal chandeliers* – and she said fervently that she wasn't ever going to do it again because the rotten sods had dropped her in it and she'd never been so frightened in her life. When she'd gone we had a bit of trouble with our consciences, but it got worse because an hour or so later one of her confederates turned up at the door, glowing with gratitude and laden with pound notes which he attempted to press upon us. We protested that it had really been no trouble at all and we couldn't possibly accept anything, but he said he wanted to make the children a little present, and the children who were much too young to entertain any sophisticated reservations about the fruits of sin grabbed it gladly. Looking back I suppose I should have taken it off them and put it in the poor box in the church, but by that time I was exhausted. Come to think of it I'm not at all sure I ever confessed it, so I'd better go and do that now.

This is known as the Lord Longford syndrome – forgiving someone for what they've done to someone other than yourself.

Tomfoolery

Every decade or so I make up my mind that now I've cracked it, that I have understood the secret of the universe, the meaning of life and the motivation behind human behaviour, and every single time it is revealed to me five minutes later that I have not. I thought, at least, that I understood the cats but they have all turned out to be not what they seemed.

The cat Cadders, whom I considered to be a terrible thug, can be charm and gentleness itself, whereas Puss whom I thought was an innocent loving creature has shown herself to be frequently devious and spiteful. She lies in wait for Cadders and makes a scene, and Cadders gets the blame. As Janet says – that cat is a cow. I have often known children to behave in this way. I suppose

most parents have found that they have punished a larger
child for biffing a smaller only to discover that the curly-
haired little one with the brimming eyes was undoubtedly
the prime aggressor. We have a nineteenth-century work
on *The Cat* by one M. Champfleury, who writes that
'Dupont de Nemours, a naturalist philosopher who was
under the direct influence of the great minds of the
eighteenth century,' suggested a method of understanding
the brute creation which was simply 'to study the animal
in ourselves.' Easier said than done, since how does one
ascertain where the one ends and the other begins, if
indeed there is a division? He goes on to quote Montaigne:
'A point undecided, and of course guesswork, is, to which
of us belongs the fault that we do not not understand
each other? For we understand them no more than they
understand us: for this same reason, they may esteem
us beasts, as we esteem them!' What? I feel that that
could have been better put, but maybe it's clearer in the
original. Anyway I don't think I agree with him. I think
cats may well model their behaviour on that of the people
around them, and have sometimes wondered uneasily
who Puss imagines she is imitating when she lies on the
window sill waving her feet seductively, only to roll off
in undignified fashion. (Being impersonated by a child
can give a nasty turn too. Recognisable bellows of 'You

just wait till I get you home' etc, can make one feel quite
sweaty.)

I once went to Marrakesh with Diana Melly, and
we stayed not in La Mamounia but in the more
modest establishment over the road, and there were
cats everywhere. They lounged round in groups, lying
in the shade on the terrace and near the swimming
pool. Every now and then one of them would go for
a little stroll or dash into the dining-room to grab a
momentarily unattended morsel. They argued very little
among themselves, although they seemed to be of all
ages, shapes and sizes. They just hung round, sort of
resting. British cats don't behave like that. They are not
gregarious; they leave their homes only to go out, as
it were, on business, and when they meet they seldom
speak. They like to hurry home and settle down by the
telly. You will sometimes find one napping under a bush
when the weather is fine but seldom in the company of
its fellows. We were fascinated by these cats since while
their demeanour seemed to us to be uncharacteristic of the
species it was also reminiscent of something else. Then it
came to us. They were behaving like tourists, like people
on holiday. The cat languorously licking his stomach was
scarcely different from the blonde by the pool rubbing
suntan lotion into hers. The cat rising to his feet and

stretching himself was precisely similar to the frenchman doing likewise on the other side of the bush. The one drinking the dregs from a cup of coffee was just like us. Their sorties into the dining-room were unlike ours only in so far as they were quicker off the mark and we were never kicked by the waiters. They exhibited the same degree of distant tolerance to each other as did the hotel guests caught in proximity in conditions of complete idleness, and it was all faintly humbling.

But the oddest bit of feline behaviour I ever witnessed occurred only the other day. Puss and the many-toed cat are both female (only Puss being spayed) and Cadders is an altered tom. One afternoon I was in the drawing-room and observed Puss raising her tail and wiggling her bum in the way that tom cats do and then she *sprayed the curtains.* I leapt to my feet thinking she must be, not Puss, but an alien male, only to find that it was undoubtedly her. I didn't know lady cats *could* do that. Then a few days later I caught the many-toed cat doing the same thing to the wastepaper basket. I can only put it down to an outbreak of feline feminism, though this still leaves me bewildered. I am just as confused by human feminism, because if you disapprove of them so much why wash off the make-up, crop the hair and slap on the boiler suit in order to resemble the rotters? No. I haven't cracked it at all.

Almost human

The daffodil was out in the London garden when we left. Just the one, looking like someone who has turned up, dressed to the nines, for a glamorous party on the wrong night. You had to admire its style, for while it looked faintly foolish it also looked gallant and insouciant, prepared to stick it out in solitary splendour. I wish now that I had done the Perfect Hostess thing and bought a pot of its fellows to keep it company. I am thinking of those people who when they see a guest committing some dreadful social solecism – peas on the knife, drinking the water in the finger bowl – do likewise. Here in Wales of course there are fields of daffodils in positively Wordsworthian profusion and they look very beautiful but not nearly so touching. I hope I am not going to start worrying about plants having feelings. Lamb chops are already off the menu because lamb chops on the hoof are gambolling outside the windows and the words 'mint sauce' have taken on menacingly brutal connotations. It would be a nuisance if one had to think up ways of anaesthetising the cabbage before plunging it into boiling water. Mrs Earl in her *Pot Pourri from a Surrey Garden* takes the view, which seems sensible while stopping short of sentimentality, that when starting a garden you should be prepared to care properly for the plants you have chosen, giving due consideration to their various requirements, respecting their idiosyncrasies and protecting them, in so far as you are able, from drought, blight, slug and the ginger tom next door. Rather like starting a family, although the problems are somewhat different.*

Cooking the beans for Sunday lunch I kept thinking of that maddening ad on television which shows a lot of wrinkled and twisted old vegetables crying their eyes out because they can't join the club, while a load of uniformly perfect but dopey peas and carrots go sailing off, rejoicing, to be frozen and consumed. Cheer up, I hear

---

*I worry about two plants which can only be described as daisy trees: that is, they look like little bushes on long stems but they grow a profusion of daisies in the summer. Fine, they look very nice. But they're supposed to last through the winter and on the whole they don't. They go brown and curl up.

myself saying. It would be beastly to end up on a plate in the supporting role of two veg to the star, roast beef. I really must watch this anthropomorphic tendency. It isn't even as if I had green fingers. Someone, being aware of this, took a hand in the garden last year and cleaned it up magnificently, pruning everything to within an inch of its life. Some of the plants, the mock orange, the weigela responded with gratitude but the albertine is still sulking and the all-encroaching ivy with gleeful spite is preparing to take over the world. We know enough to know when we haven't got it quite right so have enlisted the help of an expert, lovely Elizabeth Smart who has towards plants that kindly awareness, the casual assurance that shepherds have towards sheep and the best mothers towards their children. She knows their little ways. We have planted wisteria, clematis, purple pansies and a passion flower and I want to put in a bougainvillea because it would go so well with the balcony. I wish we could have spanish moss too but am told it would not do well in Camden Town.

In the back yard we keep a mad magnolia. Every now and then it remembers that it is supposed to have flowers and produces a few, though mostly over the neighbour's garden wall. Last year it had a bud in December which froze until it dropped off in the spring thaw, making me think of a mother taking her baby to a Christmas party clad only in cotton rompers. Should we wish to see its flowers we have to visit the neighbour, or lean dangerously far out of the bathroom window. The plants in the front garden evidence the same tendency to avoid us – the roses climbing to the right into Robin's garden while the honeysuckle favours the left, preferring to bestow itself on Alan Bennett. It is very odd because if it is the sun they are seeking it cannot possibly be on both sides at once. The new plants are in the middle of the garden and it will be interesting to see if they attempt to stray. We look forward to the summer, sitting in the shade while the scent of the blossoms, we hope, disguises the smell of cat and the odour of scorched kebab from the Greek restaurant. If the worst comes to the worst I am going to buy cut flowers from the market and keep them in a vase on the garden table.

No explanations

We had a very ecumenical Easter in the country with a number of people who were too young to have made up their minds yet on the matter of the existence of God: Janice who is Jewish, Mouness who is Muslim, Joan who is Vegetarian and Mary whose uncle holds a position at the Vatican. Mouness doubles as an agnostic because he says although he would like to be an atheist he hasn't got the bottle, which seems to me an entirely reasonable attitude. I find militant atheists rather more tiresome than charismatic Christians. They remind me of a person I knew who would strenuously deny the presence of mice in the house when you could hear them scampering in the wainscotting and eating their way through the rafters in the loft. Having stated his position he simply could not bring himself to admit that there just might be rodent-type creatures somewhere around.

Mouness's father wept at the Requiem Mass for our second son and recited a verse from the Koran over his grave, and Mouness's mother too manifests those virtues associated with true religion – gentleness, generosity, courage and magnanimity. If there were more people who actually behaved as their religion requires them to do and everyone else would shut up arguing about it we should all get along much better.

I have decided, not for the first time, to go to Mass on a more regular basis and just learn to put up with the irritants introduced by Vatican II. I am already kind to old ladies unless I hate them, and most of the commandments are fairly safe in my hands. None the less I am aware that I fall somewhat short of the requirements even of the Penny Catechism and feel uneasy in the presence of nuns, who mostly seem to have such clear perceptive eyes. I think I must go on a Retreat and get my spirit polished up. Convents are excellent places in which to take a look at yourself. No distractions and no drink to take the corners off. The spirits that come in bottles tend initially to give one rather a good conceit of oneself, and deprivation can prove very salutary, which is, I suppose, why certain saints chose to live in hermitages or up poles or to get themselves martyred. I don't intend to go that far.

Few people believe that the breathing we heard outside last summer was of supernatural origin, many claiming that it was a hedgehog. I put this theory to Alan, who was one of the witnesses, and he said it might just be possible if there were about three thousand hedgehogs ranged on the mountainside breathing in unison. It might also, of course, have been one hedgehog breathing through an amplifier, and if anyone can suggest how this concatenation of circumstances could have come about I shall accept his explanation. It was very loud and just as audible three or four hundred yards up the hill as under the damson tree.

Alfred's friend Kay recently suffered a more prosaic but more distressing domestic mystery. Her fridge blew up. She heard a dull explosion early one morning, and going to investigate found the fridge door on the other side of the kitchen and the glass in the window shattered. Everything in the body of the fridge was unharmed, but, everything in the door – eggs, milk, fruit-juice – was trickling all over the floor. She sent for a man from the shop where the fridge had come from and he turned out to be a sceptic. He kept grinning at her in a sneering, cynical sort of fashion, and all she could do, being in shock, was to point wordlessly at the evidence. She sent for the gas man too, since although it wasn't a gas-powered fridge she was just so *confused*. I asked her to lunch to tell me all about it, and when she was a bit late Alfred said worriedly that the way her luck was running she'd probably just discovered the gas stove had frozen over. We don't expect an arcane solution here, just a simple explanation from someone conversant with the laws of physics. There was no champagne in the fridge, not so much as a can of lager. Could it have been live yoghurt?

Cut short

The telephone in the country was what is politely known as 'temporarily disconnected' and even after we had rectified the omission it remained obstinately mute. This was because, as a weary telephonist explained to Janet who rang her from the village shop, it was an unmanned exchange. This phrase gave rise to ribald speculation, which gave way to rage as the phone stayed dead and we realised that until some engineer found a moment to pop in and do something about it we would remain cut off from the world.

The maddening thing was that huge yellow Telecom vehicles were trundling all over the countryside. There is nothing more infuriating than things which urge you to rely on them and then refuse to work. Had I known that in order to communicate with anyone I should have to press a peasant into running with a message in a forked stick I should have made arrangements accordingly. Nor did I know that if you telephone London from a Welsh call box 10p will now buy you precisely 30 seconds. Just long enough for you to say Hello, the other bloke to say Hello and then it goes beep beep beep. You find yourself going beep beep beep after a bit too. Anyway the call box in the village had someone else's 10p stuck irremoveably in it and the call box in the next village won't even permit you 30 seconds. The other bloke says Hello, you bang in the 10p and it goes beep beep beep *immediately*. I had to telephone a tiny little review of a book because I'd said I would and it was deadline day and I was beginning to gibber, so in the end I reversed the charges from the village shop. Unfortunately the review contained the word virginity and – worse – masturbation, and if you try and whisper on the telephone the other person can't hear you and you end up yelling. I just knew that that would be the day the Rural Dean would choose to discover that the rectory had run out of sardines or the ladies of the Women's Institute would all come in to buy sugar to make jam, so I wasn't particularly lucid and I don't suppose the review will make any sense at all.

It is difficult enough at the best of times to make

sure one's copy is error-free. I once wrote a book with the phrase 'poppies as red as pain', which I thought rather neat, and the printer went Tsk tsk, silly girl, and put 'red as *paint*'. Then I once wrote a book about baby food with some frightfully erudite aside about the causal relationship between salt and something, but printers will *never* let you say 'causal'; smiling and shaking their heads indulgently they always change it to 'casual', which does something fairly crucial to the meaning.

Back in London our fifth son – whose given name is Arthur and who has recently taken up karate and is now known in consequence as Martial Art – had taken over the kitchen table to do his O Level revision because the desk in his own room has had to be pushed under the pool table to make room for him to sleep. The daughter (who is occasionally pronounced to rhyme with laughter, because there are times when it seems apt) has added a sweetjar full of tadpoles to the general mess, so I have to prepare meals in the scullery. Flat surfaces should perhaps be banned. No one seems able to resist the compulsion to put things on them. I like to see a gleaming uncluttered table-top adorned with nothing more than a bowl of roses. Fat chance. Ours are all covered with old magazines, and the coat somebody has just removed, and snooker cues in cases. Not to mention cats.

Someone was very distressed one day to find that the damn cats had caught a bird but neglected to kill it. He sent for the first-born son on the grounds that he reads what Someone still insists on referring to as the '*Manchester Guardian*' and should therefore be prepared to cope with the merciful business of administering the *coup de grâce*, but the first-born son is even more squeamish than his papa who only reads *The Times*. He therefore resolved the matter by drowning the poor bird in a bucket, because he couldn't bring himself to wring its neck, the time-honoured method of despatching our feathered friends. So far so good, but then he couldn't think what to do with it and in a moment of inspiration slung it over the wall into Alan Bennett's garden. Next day it was back, so he approached Alan accusingly, and demanded, 'Did you throw a dead bird into my garden?' Somewhat bewildered, Alan denied it, and then the fifth son revealed that the cats had brought it back, because he had watched them doing it. Someone then threw the body over the other wall into Robin's garden, reasoning that if Robin didn't like it he could dispose of it in the garden of his next neighbour, the lady from Saatchi and Saatchi, and if she didn't like it – but the progressive possibilities are endless and I refuse to speculate further.

So to speak

The fifth son who does a bit of acting on the side was recently required to portray a juvenile delinquent for a TV series and one of the ladies organising the thing telephoned to arrange the details. Unfortunately the phone was answered by Someone whose accent is what used to be described as 'Oxford' and the lady rang the agent in a panic to enquire whether the son spoke like the father because if so he would be absolutely no use to them. The agent was able to reassure her on this point. I don't know why people are supposed to like the sounds of their own voices. Even the ones who can't stop talking, ever, go all hot and shrinking when they hear themselves on tape. I am told one's voice sounds different in one's own ears because you can hear it from inside or something. It's rather like being photographed. I know very few people who rejoice in snapshots of themselves. They never quite live up to the image that each person cherishes in his bosom.

One Sunday I was preparing lunch and listening to the wireless when I suddenly heard a perfectly awful woman yapping away and it was *me*. I knew I was going to be on at tea time but they did a sort of trailer which took me by surprise and put me off my lunch, I can tell you. I kept whimpering, 'I don't talk like that do I?' And everyone said cruelly, 'Yes, you do.' But I know I don't always because I find some accents fatally catching and return from Wales talking chi chi and going 'Look you'. When I'm talking to Alfie I say 'Gor blimey' and things and drop my aitches, which doesn't matter when it's him but can be embarrassing if it's the gas man. I can't help it. German and Swedish are catching too, but not Arab or Russian, and the two worst accents in the world are Basle and Birmingham. The fourth son had trouble in the US of A trying to order something to put on his bread. It was no use saying 'bu--er' or even 'butter'. What he wanted is called 'buddre' and unless you say it like that your bread stays dry.

I find it odd that accents can change in a lifetime. In American '40s films the actors sound the way English actors sound now trying to impersonate Americans. The Bronx has given way to California. An admirer of the fourth son rang one night from LA and woke up Someone in the small hours. She said, 'Gee your accent is so wonderful, go on talking, just say anything,' which was clever of her because normally when Someone is woken up in the small hours what he says is strangely incompatible with the Oxford accent. The oddest thing of all is what happened to the Rank (R*e*nk) starlet accent (*e*ccent). British '40s films are full of g*e*ls in h*e*ts d*e*ncing with ch*e*ps in p*e*nts, and while a lot of those starlets must still be around (though they're probably white dwarflets or collapsars by now) I bet they don't talk like th*e*t any more. I met a man the other evening who had a double-barrelled name and sounded as though he'd been born with a silver spoon in his mouth and never bothered to take it out, but while he talked more far back than anyone I can recall his *a*s stayed in place.

French too has changed. I don't meet all that many French people, but when I do I get the impression that the *r* has ceased to roll. Someone who learned French in France when he was a little boy and spoke it better than English was recently declaiming something in that language in the way he had been taught when the *r*s positively corkscrewed on the back of the tongue and the daughter said, 'Ergh, do you mind. I'm eating my dinner.'

She herself has adopted the all-purpose uni-class way of speech that all the kiddos seem to go in for now and also has a pretty hair-raising vocabulary. Sometimes her language would make a bosun blench, but I don't worry too much because I think it's just a *phase*, though I still find some of the things the children say to their teachers fairly astonishing. If I'd called any of mine anything more than 'Miss' I'd have been expelled.

Still, all these things get ironed out in the end. The older boys are now perfectly comprehensible and seldom rude to people. The eldest son was even polite to a pair of Jehovah's Witnesses who called the other day to save his soul. One was little and meek and the other was big and aggressive. The little one enquired whether the eldest son read the Bible much. The answer being in the negative, the big one asked threateningly whether Armageddon meant anything to him and *of course* when the son told his friend Mark about it Mark said he hoped the response had been, 'It sure does. Armageddon out of here.' Too late, too late. Oh the pity of it.

Coming clean

Janet says that, whereas when most people use the royal 'we' they mean 'I', when I use it I mean her — as in 'Janet, we must do the spring cleaning/worm the cats/fill in some tax forms, etc.' The sun popped out briefly the other day and Someone asked me why I didn't clean the windows. I explained that I didn't clean windows; window-cleaners cleaned windows and I wrote a column for the *Spectator*. In truth of course when the moment comes to sit down to the blank piece of paper one would prefer to clean all the windows in Wang House. The only time I feel any enthusiasm for housework is when I'm supposed to be writing something; the floors gleam, the lavatories sparkle and the washing blows on the line. Actually I wouldn't mind housework all that much if whenever I did it everyone would go out for a week and leave the rooms as beautifully fresh as I have just rendered them. It is profoundly dispiriting to find the newly cleaned sitting-room instantly full again of half-empty mugs, crumpled newspapers, muddy wellies and people.

Tidying is the worst task of all. Someone has a good method of tidying cupboards. He takes everything out of them, so we have very tidy cupboards but rather messy hallways. I, on the other hand, incline to the Irish tidy, which is to open the cupboard door gingerly, fling everything in and then swiftly shut it before everything falls out again. I *cannot* bring myself to throw anything away, which is foolish in more ways than one since if one of the family has died the house is mined with occasions of pain and looking for a pair of your gloves you will find a pair of his shoes and the grief comes flooding back, unchanged by time. I have frequently thought that the dead should be buried with all their belongings. It seems weirdly perverse that their clothes should still be here when the people you love best in the world have gone.

But then I have kept so many clothes that the wardrobe is in danger of collapsing; not only have I retained the wedding dress and the Christening robe but I have a pair of rompers which I wore as a tot, a number of maternity smocks, *all* the daughter's baby

clothes, evening frocks which went out of fashion twenty
years ago, umpteen coats and skirts which are just too
good to dispose of and a bundle of towelling nappies,
because you never know when they'll come in useful.
The floor of the wardrobe is crammed with old handbags
full of unanswered letters because, sooner than sort them
out which gives rise to intolerable guilt, every time a
handbag becomes too heavy to carry I stick it in the
wardrobe and buy a new one; and lurking in a corner
is a full-length musquash coat which is unwearable now
since it fell in half. Possessions are a terrible nuisance; if
they're nice they're asking to be stolen, and whether they're
nice or not they gather dust or get lost. Some American
university wrote to me the other day requesting my MSS
and papers, etc. What a wonderful idea. I thought with
huge enthusiasm that I could simply pile everything into
about eighteen large cardboard boxes and send it off – old
gas bills and their envelopes, all the unanswered letters, the
bits of other people's MSS which had got interleaved with
mine, the forms I'd forgotten to fill in, the old newspapers
I couldn't remember why I was keeping, train tickets,
receipts – the lot. Then I realised that in all the welter
there were undoubtedly things I wanted to keep for reasons
I couldn't remember and one day I would undoubtedly
regret losing them. Sadly I abandoned the idea and

closed the door yet again on the unspeakable sight of my 'study'.

I mislaid Jeff the other day. We went along to receive his award and everything went off swimmingly with Jeff looking immaculately beautiful in his dinner jacket. Then a lady came to whisk him off to have his picture taken and I never saw him again. The Writer of the Year had dematerialised.

I've found him again since then. He came to lunch yesterday and was struck by another aspect of the cats' behaviour. They were wandering round in a rather aimless fashion, and after observing them for a while he realised that they obviously had a deadline to meet. They would stroll into the garden to look at the flowers or suddenly remember urgent business upstairs. Cadders disappeared completely at one point and was discovered asleep in the wardrobe on the bottom half of the musquash. He was quite clearly hiding from an editor.

Modern times

I went out again last Tuesday evening, something I do as seldom as possible because I like to get to bed around 9 o'clock, but this was a special occasion – the opening of an exhibition of new work by one of my favourite painters/human beings – the Welsh painter, Kyffin Williams. I mean *the* Welsh painter because I can't think of any others offhand, not Welsh ones who paint pictures of Wales. The Welsh tradition on the whole seems to be aural and oral, rather than visual, and the Principality is littered with some real architectural horrors. It was all right as long as everyone stuck to using the indigenous materials for building; but now quite often when the house seems to be in need of repair they move out, leaving it to fall down, and build themselves a new little number from simulated brick a yard or two from the old one. I know a valley where there are two beautiful farmhouses quietly rotting while the owner lives in a neo-Georgian edifice which looks dashed silly sitting there amidst the grey granite and the green grass. It has the appearance of something that somebody had been taking somewhere, putting it down for a moment while he goes off for a cup of tea. It reminds us of the plaque in Harley Street which announces that Florence Nightingale left her hospital on this site to go off to the Crimea. 'Thoughtless, that,' muses Janet as we drive past on our way to John Lewis to buy hooks-and-eyes. 'Untidy. Though I suppose if she had to leave it somewhere Harley Street must have seemed as good a place as any.'

The necessity of travelling miles to buy hooks-and-eyes is another aspect of modern life that does funny things to the blood pressure. You can buy futons in Camden Town, and oriental rugs and Portuguese pottery and fresh ginger and leather trousers and hot samosas and dirty books and budgerigars, but no hooks-and-eyes. Haberdashers and ironmongers have ceased to trade and we have to go to John Lewis if we need a new mop-head too. The planners are plotting to build a new shopping complex all over the High Street and you can bet it won't sell hooks-and-eyes. It will sell creased cotton frocks and Peruvian woollies and

Indian bangles, and the pigeons will lodge wherever they find a toehold, the winos will pee in its portals and old chip wrappers will drift sullenly on the unexpected eddies and currents of winds that it will undoubtedly cause to form. I can't think why the planners seem to be immune to the disenchantment that the rest of the community feels in relation to their developments. Do they say to themselves, 'Oh well, maybe that wasn't so successful, but we'll get it right next time.' Are they just hopelessly optimistic? I can see that the prospects of gain must colour their motives, but it doesn't seem quite that simple. I have a nasty feeling that they *believe* in what they're doing. There is a proselytising air somewhere, as though they know what's best for us and if we don't like it that's all very regrettable but hardly their fault.

There is also a chill rumour abroad that our local bakery is about to close down. It's a small shop which has been there for years and years and only once in living memory have I been the only customer present. This was by some odd fluke, since it is usually jammed with people buying crusty twists and large wholemeals and seedcake, and millers stagger in from the street with sacks of flour, saying 'Mind your backs,' and a dusty person with muscular forearms and a white hat and apron stands there to receive them. In the winter if you time it right you can buy bread hot from the oven and stuff it under your coat to temper the blasts from the development sites. There used to be a large grocer's shop next door to it where they made their own sausages – real ones that used to burst on contact with the hot frying pan – but they closed down soon after a fire in the shop on the other side half cooked all the tinned goods. We bought some cans of hot dogs for a kiddos' birthday party and when my mother opened one a stream of putrefaction shot up into her hair and all over her glasses. She wasn't half cross. I would have forgiven them that because they had wheels of farmhouse cheese and real black pudding too, but the shop is now two new shops. They sell watches that tell you the date and play tunes in one and video cassettes in the other. Our neighbour Gwynne came in yesterday for a drink, and not to waste any time he brought a gadget that stores his articles in itself, and because they stood in need of transmitting he put some little rubber muffles on the telephone and his gadget chattered away in gadgetese to some fellow gadget; which is jolly clever, and a flying leap for technology, but what I want to know is why is it so damn difficult to buy hooks-and-eyes?

Brazilian soap

Is there a Brazilian in the house? Because I want to know what happens to Isaura the Slave Girl. I can't stand the suspense. It's a Brazilian TV soap opera dubbed into English, and Portuguese must be fearfully flowery because to keep up with the lip movements the English actors have to say lines like 'It is extraordinarily courteous of you to honour me by entertaining me in your elegant and well-appointed home, famed in song and story.' Isaura herself is a tiresome girl with more than a hint of five o'clock shadow; the villain, Leoncio, is purest Sir Jasper and makes J. R. seem rather sweet. In this house everything stops at 4.30 and we gather round the set, rivetted. The fascination of the thing lies principally in the fact that it doesn't seem to have any rules: and if it does it breaks them. It went off at a dogleg the other week when the hero got burnt to a crisp. We couldn't believe it. We waited to hear that it was all a misunderstanding, that he and the virtuous lady who chanced to be with him at the time had been momentarily captured by brigands or had suffered a lapse of memory – but no, they had been definitively incinerated. The characters change character too. There's one lady who began as a raucous, grasping tart, became a golden-hearted tart and is now a modest and maidenly tart. It *is* confusing; and also, as in *Othello*, it only needs one person of moderate sense to step up and explain a few matters, point out a few very obvious facts, and all the trouble would be over. But then I don't suppose there'd be much drama if the protagonists had any sense.

I feel faintly guilty living in London and never going to the theatre, because I must be taking up space that an ardent theatregoer would be delighted to fill. I don't like Hyde Park either, or Madame Tussaud's; I detest Oxford Street and Park Lane; I can never find a taxi outside the Ritz in the evening; I can't stand Punch and Judy shows; and music makes me cough. Years and years ago Fritz Spiegl took me to an opera in Liverpool and, although when I went in I was in prime condition, after a few bars of whatever it was I was coughing my head off and people were trying to give me barley sugar. Afterwards we went to some reception at the Bluecoat building and a large prima donna called Edith was cavorting about on the dance floor. As she passed, making expansive gestures she (I trust) by inadvertence struck me on the side of the head; so I don't like opera singers much either.

Nothing changes. I was taken to the ballet quite recently, again in the best of health. It was a modern ballet and began with about thirty people lying on the stage. After some minutes they all got up and jumped a bit and then they all lay down again and I began to cough.

Television doesn't make me cough and if it did I should merely have to go to the medicine cupboard and take a mouthful of Fisherman's Friend. So I don't go out. Not even to the cinema. The last time I went to the cinema I saw someone being blown to bits in vivid technicolour and I didn't like it. If it's TV you can turn it off, but if you're in the cinema you have to sit with your eyes shut and your fingers in your ears and you feel silly. I once saw a film called *Frenzy* because Alfred Hitchcock elected to shoot it in our old office building in Covent Garden, and I watched a perfectly nice lady being graphically wronged and then throttled and I didn't like that at all. When I see a poster outside a cinema announcing that the film within offers the most terrifying experience of your life I say thanks for telling me and go off to see *The Sound of Music*. Actually I *hate The Sound of Music*. For some reason the heroine makes me think of someone who's been carved out of shoe polish. She has a peculiar quality of oleaginous angularity.

I don't think I'm a spectator by nature. I can't bear watching people leaping round on the high wire or balancing plates on poles or eating fire; the whole thing seems pregnant with disaster and most ill-advised. We went to Lord's yesterday to watch Someone playing Real Tennis, which also looks rather dangerous, with a fiercely fast and hard ball. There were a number lying around on the court and Janet remarked dreamily '*What* a lot of balls,' but she didn't really mean that because long after I had grown restive and started wanting my lunch she was leaning eagerly forward trying to grasp the rules. She tried to explain to me what she had learned, but while I could see that both the gentlemen were very good at what they were doing, precisely what it was I couldn't tell you.

In the field

Since spraying became less prevalent the wild flowers have returned in abundance and it is no longer sufficient to be able to distinguish a daisy from a buttercup. All along the lane to our house in Wales the banks are still covered with primroses and violets, which have now been joined by the greater stitchwort, ground ivy and cuckoo flower. I know this because we grew ashamed of our ignorance and so spent many hours drifting up and down with a book identifying everything that showed its face. It is exquisitely pleasurable to be able to tell a visitor from the city that that little pink flower is not red campion as he might have supposed but herb-robert because the one has basal stalks and oval leaves and the other has triangular, 1–2 pinnated leaves. In the spring the woods by the road to Sweeney Mountain were carpeted fence to fence with wood anemones, and we used to make special trips to look at them, as the Japanese go to see the cherry blossom. Now the fields round the village are full of buttercups, the roads edged with cow parsley and the slopes of the hill opposite the house blurred with bluebells. We ourselves have a splendid crop of nettles. Maldwyn sprays them occasionally, but they seem to enjoy it. On the other hand a Welsh poppy has seeded itself under the house wall and this year we caught the crab apple in blossom for the first time. I intend to plant more fruit trees one day, but the earth skims the rock the way skin skims the shin bone and I shall have to get some friable loam from somewhere. I shall also have to fence them off from the sheep who seem to eat absolutely everything except the nettles. (Even the farmer seemed a bit dazed at the power of the nettles. We were chatting away and looking at the field and they appeared to grow as we spoke.)

One day we went to see Kyffin in his house by the Straits. This necessitates a drive over the Berwyns and a trip along a stretch of lane with a hedge which he tells us is known as Jack Price's Folly, after the person who was inspired to plant it. It is formed of spiraea and looks very pretty, but the purpose of a hedge is to prevent too much egress and ingress of the stock and this hedge is

about as difficult to broach as a bead curtain. We took
the side road through the meadows and then the road
to Llyn Ogwen, and we said what we always say – that
the extraordinary thing about this part of Wales is how
the landscape changes completely every five miles or so,
from pastoral calm to frightening bleakness and back again.
As we approached Bethesda the air was unusually clear
and the sun bright, and the mountains looked oddly one-
dimensional like a backdrop. They have made a number of
films round here pretending that it's India or China, but
today for some reason it felt exactly like the Wild West,
and as we bowled along the valley bottom we thought how
utterly detestable it would be if we were being pursued by
Red Indians and how fortunate we were to be threatened
by nothing more annoying than the Jehovah's Witnesses
who had suddenly appeared in droves in Pen-y-Bont
Fawr. They didn't just stay there either. They came and
banged on the doors of people's houses and they brought
their little kiddies. The third son, idly curious, got into
conversation with some of them. They were outside the
pub at the time, so he asked his friend in a whisper if he
thought they drank. 'Absolutely not,' his friend answered
him. 'Have a drink,' invited the son confidently. 'Thanks
very much,' they responded. He was *furious*, especially
when they told him they were all going to heaven and

he wasn't. 'Do you mean to tell me,' he demanded, 'that there'll be a few hundred of you in paradise and all the rest of us will be roasting in hell?' 'Yes,' they said.

I do find some people's beliefs very curious, but you can't help envying their confidence.

Kyffin's house is called after the wild fennel (fanogl) that grows all round, and the ideal is to catch a local fish and grill it wrapped in the local herb. He grows periwinkles too and Japanese honeysuckle, and Janet and I, who may be getting rather boring on the subject, plodded round naming all the things we could identify. On the way back to London we kept passing those fields of astonishing yellow and asking each other whether it was mustard or rape. Janet said one way of telling would be to try some and see whether it made us hot or cross. Back home a newly planted rhododendron had gone from a rather attractive budding stage to being distinctly overblown. Catching sight of it unawares it made me feel homesick for Wales because it very much resembles a dead sheep.

Country life

One of the things I like about the country is that the problems it presents are different. For instance while the drain in London sometimes gets blocked up it is never because there is a hedgehog in it. This happened last summer, and by the time we located the cause of the trouble the poor creature was coated in detergent foam and half drowned, because it hadn't thought of climbing out of the drain, which is not deep, but had sought to preserve itself by curling up into a ball. I think hedgehogs are possibly dumber even than sheep, but they are more likeable. They come at night to steal the cats' food from the step and when we open the door they scuttle away like little old winos discovered rifling dustbins. Hearing a clanking one night the third son went bravely out in his underpants, air gun at the ready, and five hedgehogs loped away looking embarrassed – not, I think, at the sight of the son, but because they had been apprehended. This son shot a mouse one night earlier in the year and demanded that we photograph him standing with his foot on it. He shot a beetle too a few nights ago, which I find rather reprehensible but skilful. I said I thought it was extremely mean to shoot beetles and he said indignantly that I hadn't seen the beetle: it had come bursting in through his window like a Thing from outer space and had attempted to terrorise him all night. He said it was *huge*, so we said where was it, and it had gone. I suppose it might have recovered and flown away, but I suspect the cats ate it.

Janet is quite a good mouser. I act as beater until the rodent is cornered and she seizes it in a dish cloth. One, however, once managed to lie low until we had all gone away and it subsisted until we returned on an old forgotten potato, a five-year-old pace-egg, the bottoms of the cupboard doors and a plastic bottle of Tipp-Ex. The cats do not catch house mice. They catch field mice and bring them, living, into the house. They then ignore them and we have to catch them ourselves. The fifth son recently rescued a shrew from one of them and it sank its teeth into his finger and hung there. He was annoyed at its ingratitude and astounded at its stupidity. He had another unpleasant experience due to the cats' waywardness. One had dropped a mouse into a wellington boot where it had died. He put in his foot, felt something wriggling and discovered a bundle of maggots. You must *always* turn wellington boots upside down and shake them. One day I inserted a bare foot into one and encountered a colossal cockroach.

On one occasion Puss did kill a mouse in the house. It was a pregnant mouse and she had sort of unzipped it and laid a row of pink embryo mice on the hall floor, which was quite awful, being at once poignant and disgusting. Puss is a fairly bright animal, but sometimes her intelligence deserts her. It did last night. We had gone out to dinner and there was a cloudburst. The third son and his Mary were babysitting the daughter and suddenly noticed water seeping under the kitchen door because the drain was blocked with magnolia leaves. They then noticed Puss standing at the door on her hind legs, waist-deep in rain, not having thought to climb the magnolia. Mary had to dry her in a towel. (You can't dry a hedgehog in a towel. You can only give it warm milk and water and hope for the best.)

Erring in the opposite direction, my mother's cat, a remarkably beautiful but perverse beast, was staying with us in the country and suddenly disappeared. We could hear her miaowing for two days and the daughter and I nearly went mad looking for her. We didn't think to look *up* until the third day and there she was, about a mile up a pine tree, roosting on a branch like a hen. The builder had to bring a ladder to get her down and he was extraordinarily brave because the pine was growing on a steep and shingly slope.

It is very disconcerting to find animals in unexpected places. Last year we stopped at a garage for some petrol and there was a tiger sitting in a sort of chicken coop. I think it was an advertising stunt, but it made us feel nervous. Then just a few days ago on the way home we saw an odd-looking animal digging in a field with its tail curled over like a croquet hoop. It was a squirrel. I said perhaps it had mistaken itself for a mole. The daughter said it was probably trying to remember where it had buried its nuts. And Janet, who really does not in the least resemble the popular or accepted image of your average English nanny, said that that would certainly account for the peculiar angle of its tail.

An uninvited guest

She walked idly under the overhanging branches of the weigela, pushed open the gate with a nonchalant hand and, humming a light air, stepped into the garden. Then she stood, suddenly still, aghast. For there before her astounded gaze . . .

Enough of that. Anyway it wasn't her, it was me, and what lay before my astounded gaze was a filthy large stranger in a mac curled up on the mat outside the front door, fast asleep. I crept into the house through the laundry door and I said to Janet in a shocked whisper, 'There's a drunk in the garden,' and Janet said, 'So what's new?' I said that there was all the difference in the world between a drunken friend in the garden and a drunken stranger and added that I didn't care at all for the look of this one. The sons were all for picking him up and throwing him out, but when I had roughly described his dimensions and the overall cut of his jib they decided against it. Besides there is always something vulnerable about sleeping people, and while I could see that it would not be appropriate to wake him with a cup of tea and a copy of *The Times*, I could see no reason for physical violence. He was only asleep after all.

Then as the afternoon wore on we realised that the daughter would soon be home and might not take too kindly to the unexpected presence, so we telephoned the police and put the problem to them. An amiable officer said indulgently that it was probably only a wino, and we said we knew that and we didn't want to make a fuss but we found him inconvenient, so he said he'd send someone round and we waited. While we waited the sleeper awoke in a confused and disoriented state and attempted to leave by climbing down the wall into the dug-out part of the garden, so we rang the police again and said he was clumping all over the morning glories now and we were getting a bit fed up, and the policeman assured us that an officer was on his way. So we hung up and waited. While we waited the stranger finally located the gate and went out, but not far, because he clearly regretted this move and kept coming back, opening the gate and peering

round, whereupon all the inhabitants of the house would
fling up their respective windows and screech at him to
go away. This went on for some time. There was still no
sign of the police officer and I suggested that perhaps
we should go out and double-park the car, at which they
would be upon us in droves. The police are rather like
taxi cabs in that there's never one around when you want
one (sometimes within feet of home if I see a taxi with its
lights on I have to go to some lengths to prevent myself
hailing it simply because it's there). Most days I practically
trip over policemen strolling along in pairs, and I always
smile at them nicely, because they make me feel guilty.
Priests have rather the same effect. And headmistresses.
If Janet sails insouciantly through a red light there's
usually a policeman to observe her. Whole forces hang
around outside pubs, and they spend a lot of time asking
questions of naughty-looking passers-by, but when a local
restaurateur brandishing a meat-cleaver threatened to put
the fifth son in a stew there wasn't a policeman for miles.

Eventually the stranger drifted away around the corner,
but I couldn't relax because a new worry had occurred to
me. Someone would shortly be returning from a convivial
lunch at Bertorelli's. He had left wearing a mac so there
was a ten per cent chance that he would return in it.
Should the police arrive in expectation of finding a merry

person in a mac it was entirely possible that they would not be disappointed.

There is a great deal of drunkenness round here in one way or another. The most spectacular examples take place in the doorways in the market where men and women break their fast on sherry and cider and continue drinking all day, mostly in a spirit of comradeship, shaking hands when one of their number leaves and wishing him God speed but occasionally falling out and howling at each other. I don't know how they would do this if it were not for the existence of that word with which they preface all others and which is frequently employed as both verb and noun. When addressing other members of the public however they are usually polite, asking nicely if one would lend them the loan of thirty pence for a bag of chips, and while I know perfectly well that they have no intention of buying chips but are saving up for a bottle of VP wine I can never see how a refusal would be justified since there is always the possibility that they really *do* intend to buy a packet of chips.

The way to Wales

I know the way to Wales. I'm not sure that I could find my way to Leicester Square, unless I took a taxi, but I know the way to Wales because we go there so often, and although it is Janet who does the driving I like to keep on the alert, ever since the time she fell asleep round Birmingham. I know two ways to Wales. I know the way through Towcester where there is a most excellent chip shop and ten miles further on is a jolly good pub called the Narrow Boat where they sell real food as opposed to whatever it is they have on offer in the Motorway Caff, where even the salt is tasteless. In the Narrow Boat they serve real steak and kidney pud. I hate kidneys but I approve of their presence in steak and kidney pud because of the Trades Description Act. I fish them out and take

them away for Cadders, who loves them. And I know the
scenic route which passes through Chipping Norton.

My friend the psychoanalyst drove us to Wales the
other weekend. I said I knew two ways, and which would
he prefer, but he was determined to find a way of his own.
I kept bleating about the Vale of Evesham and Wyre Piddle
and he told me to shut up and not be so silly. He scribbled
a route on the map and gave it to his mother so she could
navigate and we set off on a very circuitous journey. Every
so often she would mildly suggest a small deviation from
his chosen route and this made him cross. At one point
he removed a hand from the wheel and jabbed irritatedly
at the map with his forefinger. 'It's *that* effing road,' he
remarked, 'you daft old bat,' a phrase which seems to me
to be deficient in both filial respect and professional polish
– but then we're none of us perfect and, by dint of driving
like the clappers, he got us to our destination before
nightfall, despite an interesting circular tour of Ludlow.

Two of the boys have just set off complete with ruck
sacks and ghetto-blaster to travel by train and the weekly
bus and I wonder if they'll ever get there. In the old days
before Dr Beeching modernised the railways the train
went straight to our village and we have a pub called
the Railway Inn which puzzles strangers very much since
the nearest length of track is thirty miles away. I am

also wondering what the weather is doing down there since they still have a few miles to walk from the bus stop to the house and are not wearing mackintoshes. It is most certainly raining here. It was raining there over the weekend and I kept trying to convince myself that it wasn't. It is maddening to track hundreds of miles to the country merely to huddle indoors, which one can do more comfortably in London anyway, and the guilt of the hostess is almost insupportable. Irrational, indeed absurd, but when the rain streaks out of the sky in an undifferentiated mass she feels it is her fault. She bleats about how lovely it was last week when the periwinkles were at their best and it was seventy in the shade, but it doesn't make much difference to the prevailing discomfort. The house becomes miserable with mud; damp condenses on the windows; people go virtuously for walks because it *is* the country, after all, and that's what it's for; and when they return with earache they sit by a sullenly smoking fire and play Frustration. The hostess feels it incumbent on her, given the circumstances, to make large hot meals instead of easy cold picnics and this makes her cross, and it is only as dusk descends and the promising sound of popping corks is heard that everyone is able to relax.

We sat in the garden in the wind and the rain, and the analyst cleaned his motor car and played his violin while

I read aloud from the Book of Judges, not because it was Sunday but because Judges 19 describes a journey even more hellish than the one we had just undergone. (It had been worse for me because I had insisted on bringing the plate rack and it stuck in the back of my neck the whole way.) The travellers in Judges 19 must have most fervently wished that they had stayed at home. I won't relate here what happened to them, because it is actually too horrible. Suffice it to say that one poor girl ended up being chopped into twelve pieces and posted off into all the coasts of Israel, and that wasn't the worst thing. What is particularly interesting is that there is a strong hint that all the trouble only happened because the male traveller kept allowing himself to be seduced into having just one more for the road. The biblical for this is 'I beseech thee to take a little meat; and strengthening thyself, till the day be further advanced; afterwards thou mayest depart', or 'Tarry with me today also and spend the day in mirth'. It is a perfectly awful warning of what can happen to the weak-willed, and also a reminder that travel can be vastly overrated.

Table d'Hôte

I have decided that, like it or not, I *must* go to Mass again every Sunday. I gave it up when one day some years ago I walked unsuspectingly into our local church to find the congregation giving a spirited rendering of Shall We Gather at the River. And they had painted the interior white and flung out the holy statues. Only very small chapels should be painted white, and I don't really mind if they have stripped-pine benches and the nuns have invited a local artist to render his own conception of Our Lady in bog oak or polystyrene or whatever his chosen medium may be. At least, I do mind a bit — artistic appreciation is a tricky business — but I can take it on a small scale. The local church is quite a roomy edifice, with a vaulted ceiling and a side chapel, and when it was all white it looked rather like Alaska and made one feel unwelcome and huddle into one's coat. The parish church should be warm and darkly glowing, with a sanctuary light – and I don't give a hoot what anyone else thinks.

My friend the regular churchgoer took me along with him last Sunday, cautiously choosing the moment to avoid the Country and Western Mass or any possible Pet Blessing, and allowing me time to put the roast in the simmering oven to rest. They have repainted the interior now in rather pleasant shades of apricot and banana; there is a thoroughly satisfying statue of Our Lady on the right, and several brightly-coloured saints have returned to their various niches. The side chapel by some happy coincidence has been painted in the same blue as I have painted my back kitchen. It is a shade at once innocent and vulgar, by which I mean it makes absolutely no pretensions at tastefulness. I have a statue of the Sacred Heart in my back kitchen, and a rather good picture of Therèse of Lisieux, who seems to get proportionately less sickening as one grows older, a small bronze of Our Lady of Victories and a ceramic of St Anne and the Virgin as a child. For some reason they seem perfectly at home in the kitchen while they would look deuced odd in the drawing-room, so I have to admit that churches and kitchens have something in common and it must, of course, be to do with Holy

Communion. On the other hand, now the priest faces the congregation it gives an incongruous impression of hotel dining-room; one sees too much of all the napery and the utensils; the celebrant seems less sacerdotal than menial, more like a napkin-flapping *maître d.* than someone communicating with his God. The symbolism has gone awry. Once the priest, back to the congregation, faced outwards, towards eternity, and raised the cup to the Lord. Now he and the congregation gaze on each others' ugly mugs and the raising of the chalice seems more like a toast than anything else. I do so wish people wouldn't meddle. The old Mass had got it right. It seems absolutely mad to have it in the vernacular at a time in history when more people are travelling than ever before, and whereas once an RC anywhere would be at home with the Latin now he has to sit through Walloon or Cree or Gaelic. All that promiscuous shaking of hands is a hopelessly hypocritical bit of top dressing and quite unsuited to the British, who have stinking manners anyway (it seems more natural in, say, Bruges where the people traditionally and habitually shake hands on meeting, or parting, or before going to bed) and some of the things they now say make me go all hot.

The phrase which in particular drives me insane is the one about our 'spiritual drink'. For one thing, if that isn't a nod in the direction of consubstantiation then my theology is even creakier than people keep telling me. And for another, all that stuff about fruit of the vine, gathered by human hands, etc, has a horrid echo of the worst sort of menu – the salad of your choice, dawn-gathered for your delectation and served in individual portions. But the worst thing of all is that, as a housewife, I am extremely suspicious of the word 'drink' used in that context. If I pick up a bottle labelled orange drink I put it contemptuously aside because it is not the real thing: it may have had some glancing acquaintance with the citrus in question, but it is not pure juice. 'Drink' is a word the manufacturers use when they want to put one over on you. So, I ask myself, worrying about blasphemy, is that the blood of Christ or is it not? Or is it merely Christ-flavoured with added colourants and stabilizers and BF8X?

I think we should be told.

River-boat ride

The summer party season is at its height and I'm
wondering how many people have OD'd on white wine.
I have. I never want to see another spoonful of fermented
grape juice, especially now that we're told it's full of anti-
freeze. Apparently they add it to wine to sweeten it, which
seems most peculiar. It would not occur to one, after all,
to put it in one's tea in lieu of the lump of sugar or the
saccharine tablet. My stomach is now behaving like an
animal which has been ill-treated by its owner and refuses
to trust anything I offer it. It will grudgingly accept the
occasional Marie biscuit, but nothing more. I felt quite
ill the other day so I lay on my back and Cadders lay on
my stomach (cats are preferable to hot water bottles in
that their covers do not slip off and they don't go cold)

and I vowed not to go to any more parties ever. Then my oldest chum, Zélide, came along with an invitation to the barge race, which was quite irresistible. We boarded the vessel *Naticia* at Greenwich pier and joined a group of lightermen and their families and sailed up and down the Thames watching young men *rowing* these colossal barges. I had my money on the large one covered with coloured hearts, but it kept getting athwart the tide and the Virgin Atlantic barge won. I had been told by two friends that the best thing to placate an indignant stomach is port-and-brandy, so I drank a few of those and had a very enjoyable time. Zélide is extremely knowledgeable about matters nautical and the most observant person I have ever met, so I learned a lot about the river – most of it disheartening. Where there were warehouses there are now 'luxury homes and leisure complexes', and all the rivermen are close to despair. The barge race is intended partly to publicise the possibilities of river transport, but our host told us glum tales of warehousing ventures which were rendered redundant before completion because of ever-newer containering techniques. The egregious EEC, it seems, is responsible for this decline. Between the Americans and the Europeans the people are beginning to feel they cannot call their soul their own.

Zélide pointed out one large difference between

the lower and the upper classes in this country. Our
companions had perfect manners. They introduced us to
everyone meticulously and were careful of our comfort,
explaining the more esoteric points of barge-racing and
buying us drinks. Quite unlike, said Zélide repressively, the
people at the last party she was at, where everyone talked
over her head about Biffy and Squiffy and if you hadn't
just come galloping in from the Quorn you were beneath
notice. At one point she got so fed up she thumped her
tiny fist on the table and announced to the guests flanking
her on right and left that they had spent the entire meal
talking across her about people she had never met and she
was bored. Somewhat taken aback, they asked if she had
ever known the Dunn Witterings in Singapore and when
she said she hadn't they resumed their dialogue. I put it all
down to in-breeding.

Passing Rotherhithe we observed a wide open space
permitting a breathtaking view of some high-rise dwellings
and remembered when that space had been occupied
by a row of seventeenth-century sea-captains' houses.
Most of them were owned and lived in by people who
were prepared to cast themselves into penury in order
to maintain and care for them, but the powers that be
for some arcane reason of their own had decided that
they must be razed to the ground. Letters to *The Times*,

questions in the House, impassioned pleadings were all to no avail. Those tall, lovely houses with their panelling evocative of ships' cabins, and their little crow's-nest balconies overlooking the river were all utterly demolished and squashed. Don't worry, said the fiend in authority who held the ultimate responsibility for the act – they were going to put up concrete bollards all along the denuded waterfront to preserve the nautical quality of the area. Oh, good. So that's all right then. I had to have quite a few more port-and-brandies before I regained my composure. Still, apart from these chilling reminders of the Englishman's iniquity to his heritage, we had a heavenly time. Zélide made me look at the sky because from the river you can see all of it, and she made me look at the water because no two waves are ever quite the same and the surface of the river is not monotonous but infinitely variable. I believe I should be content to ford the Styx with Zélide because, while I was cowering in the gunwales sucking my thumb, she would notice something interesting about the traditional weave of Charon's jersey and his individual method of poling his boat.

Trading insults

I find people who express themselves as insulted very much more tiresome than those who insult people. Rudeness is annoying, but offended flouncing is worse, being so dreadfully conceited. Just think of the words 'How dare you speak to me like that'. Why ever not, you ask yourself? Who you? When I was very young I read a book which contained a phrase about people who were to be found crying on their bed because of that awful thing you said to them at lunch. It made a great impression on me at the time and now if people are nasty to me I am nasty back, rather than allowing the eyes to well over with tears, or running from the room. Someone excelled himself at a party last week by insulting a Jesuit, something I would have thought quite difficult to accomplish in view of that Order's reputation for suavity and worldliness. He said, in a friendly fashion, 'I hear you're a Jesuit,' to which the response came 'That is the truth.' Whereupon Someone cheerily remarked, 'Well, if it's the truth, you can hardly be interested in it, being a Jesuit.' The offended cleric shot away in a rage, almost walking on people in his haste to get to the front door. While feeling no sympathy for the chap, I was curious to know why Someone had felt it necessary to say what he did say and he explained in plaintive tones that he simply couldn't help himself. It was like playing a half volley off the side wall at Rackets. There was the ball: there was nothing to do but hit it – back on to the wall from whence it came: it was instinctive, it was second nature, it was irresistible.

I do see. I was once at a party when a diplomat stormed out. He was an American diplomat and somebody said something disparaging about one of his precious missiles, so he grabbed his hat (he was the sort of American who wears a hat) slammed it on his head and marched out. I said I had the impression that he'd seen somebody doing that in a film and had been waiting for an opportunity to do it himself, but everyone else said that that was doing him too much justice: he just hadn't studied hard enough at diplomacy school.

The subject of American missiles is useful if you

should find yourself unbearably bored at a dinner party. You can bring a table to uproar merely by uttering the words 'Greenham Common'. No more is needed. The rights and wrongs of it seem to be immaterial; just the word 'peace', followed by the word 'women', will induce transports of temper in men in suits.

Another good method is to announce that you have just had a most elevating chat with your aunt. You then divulge that she has been dead for some time and you have spent the afternoon with a Medium. Most of the ladies present will tend to be interested and sympathetic and possibly offer experiences of their own. They will very shortly be shouted down by the gentlemen who will probably grow quite insulting, especially if they have been to Oxford or Cambridge. Belief in the paranormal is, for some reason, taken by a lot of educated gents as a personal affront. Scientists especially get really steamed up, and their cultivated manner suffers severely. All you need to do is maintain an air of quiet certainty. To all their denials, their explanations of why such things are impossible you respond with a calm smile and a pitying shake of the head (we all know how maddening that is) and if no one has apoplexy somebody will surely storm out. The odd thing is that they will almost certainly vote Conservative. I suppose the Left has to be tolerant of so many things that one more makes no difference.

Of course if the men are wearing fisherman's jerseys and jeans and you are eating bean-and-tofu salad rather than filet de boeuf en croute, and drinking Rioja rather than Mouton Cadet, then you must change your tactics. You can say that you are planning to remove your children from the local Comprehensive in order to send them to a fee-paying convent school, or you can say you think it unwise to let paedophiles run youth groups, but for some reason it is much more difficult to make the Left cross than it is the Right. They may look a bit sullen or attempt to point out to you the error of your ways, but they seldom reach the spectacular heights of screaming wrath that a Tory can achieve. I wonder why this is.

Baby talk

I was sitting quietly in the drawing-room yesterday evening when I heard somebody calling my name in the garden, so I stepped on the balcony and there below was a total stranger. 'Yers?' I said — my habitual mode of address to strangers. He accused me of not recognising him and I had to admit that he was right, whereupon he reminded me that I was engaged to him, or rather that I had been some years before. Hearing this, I invited him in and gave him a drink. He said that I had hardly changed at all, though since as the evening progressed and we indulged in reminiscence he went on to say dreamily that I had been a horrible mess I was not as flattered as I might have been. A touch scatty perhaps, but a terrible mess? Never. He made me feel a bit guilty, because he had bought a barge for us to live on and when I hopped it the rotten thing sank. Still, it was a long time ago and I think he's got over it. He's a very nice man and I still can't remember why I didn't marry him. He told the daughter that he had once loved her mother very much, and she looked amazed.

It's been a fairly nostalgic week all round. My dear friend Gully popped in on her way from New York to France, bringing her little baby. We sat in the garden and it all came back to me. When babies get off their bottoms and start crawling, one can do absolutely nothing but *watch* them like a hawk every single minute they're awake. Take your eyes off them for a second and they're experimenting with the dietary possibilities of earthworms – or worse. This particular baby was very partial to dirty little stones, and her mother leapt up and down through the whole course of a hot afternoon, persuading Rebecca to 'spit it out in Mummy's hand' – a phrase as familiar to me as 'good night' or 'good morning'. When she wasn't consuming nameless bits and pieces the baby was trying unsuccessfully to befriend Cadders or scaling the garden steps. She was a very clean baby when she arrived, but when she left she wasn't. She also preferred her marmite sandwich with a rich admixture of earth. I reflected again that it's a miracle how the small creatures survive and remembered with some awe that at one time we had four little boys under five and no one to help, since at that time Janet would only have been ten.

Some of my friends are longing to be grandmamas (come to think of it some of my friends *are* grandmamas), but I have put it around the family that while I will be enchanted to entertain any possible little ones to the occasional tea I will not be available for extended summer holidays as, to coin a phrase, I have had babies. I vividly recall an occasion when the eldest son was starting to crawl. We were sitting in a garden in the country with acres of velvet lawn and I picked him up and ran with him, dropped him on the touch line and flew back to sip a drink in comparative peace before he could get at me again. He came thundering over the lawn on his hands and knees and peed on Randolph Churchill who had ill-advisedly taken him on to his lap. I can't imagine why. It was a most uncharacteristic gesture – on the part of R. Churchill, I mean, not of the son. There's nothing you can say, really. Apology seems inadequate and explanation otiose. My cousin Pansy was once on a bus with her baby when he suddenly and without warning threw up in the brim of the hat of the lady in front. My cousin said nothing – what *can* you say? 'My baby's been sick in your hat'? It sounds stupid. Anyway, she simply got off the bus at the next stop, bang in the middle of the wastes of the North Wales littoral and waited for an hour or three for the next bus. I would have done exactly the same thing myself.

There is, however, one broody creature in the house. Puss cannot differentiate between socks and kittens. We could never understand why, each morning, there were bundles of socks not in the laundry but littered (*littered*) round the kitchen. Then one night going downstairs to investigate a strange noise, or raid the fridge or something, I caught her with a rolled-up sock in her mouth. She was carrying it, head high, with that mixture of pride, tenderness and responsibility that cats evince when moving their babies to a place of safety. I cried. We have had her spayed, so she can't have any more kittens, and I felt like the most awful monster.

I think I'm going to cry again.

Thick and thin

Eat, drink and be merry, for tomorrow we diet. These words seemed to hang in the air last week as Janet and I planned an assault course on our persons. I had been told of this diet which gives you all the nutrition the body requires while having the same reducing effect as starvation. Well, today we started on it. You take, three times daily, a bowl of a sort of thinnish gruel in various flavours which while not actually nauseating sure ain't too delicious.

'Never mind,' I said comfortingly. 'You're allowed to add a spoonful of curry powder to it sometimes.'

'Ooh,' said Janet gloomily. 'Curried minestrone. Sounds really nice.'

No nibbling, no fruit juice, no alcohol. Black

decaffeinated coffee is permitted, and unsweetened tisanes, and you have to drink a lot of water. Lord, how I hate water, especially the stuff that comes out of London taps. I forget the statistics about how many kidneys it has passed through, but they don't endear it to me. Besides we have lead pipes bearing it into the house, so I think it's dangerous. I never touch it normally. The odd thing is that after two bowls of the gruel I feel as high as a kite. Fasting has this effect on me, but I haven't been fasting. I believe Janet is rather envious as it's had no effect on her at all. 'Just think,' she says. 'We can look forward to another bowlful of this tonight.'

I hope I am not giving the impression that Janet and I are at present grossly proportioned. We are not, but some of our frocks are a bit snug and we can't afford to buy new ones. We had a lodger once who went up and down like an air-cushion and it cost him a fortune having his clothes altered by a tailor. He was forever having his trousers taken in or let out and he had hundreds of shirts in different collar-sizes. Weight is a very peculiar thing. I can still get into the jodhpurs which I wore when I was fifteen but my wedding dress barely covers the front of me. It fits the daughter perfectly, except for being a bit roomy round the bosom, and she only weighs eight stone. When we married, Someone and I both weighed nine stone and I considered myself fat and him skinny. I don't understand. Another mystery is that my wedding shoes (gold-sequinned sandals, very tasteful) will now go nowhere near my feet. No one ever told me that one's feet grow after the age of 21. My hands are the same size as they always were, but then I don't walk on them. Perhaps all these years of plodding round on one's feet makes them swell, and I don't believe any amount of dieting will turn them back into size threes. I don't care either.

The worst thing about dieting, apart from the fact that it is possible to be extremely boring on the subject, is that it disinclines one from cooking for other people. I really have no desire to toss together a delicious little boeuf bourguignon for the family while I sit lapping my gruel, so we may all end up rather thin.

The third son has just returned from Italy and tells me of a fellow guest, a girl, who resolutely refused to eat the local produce, insisting on bacon and egg and hamburgers and chips. He says her hosts got a bit fed up with her, as I can well imagine they might; but they were not altogether surprised as there is a local legend about the time just after the war when a trainload of British soldiers got snowbound in some pass. After many days a relief train arrived bearing great vats of spaghetti and they all, starving as they were, refused to eat it on the grounds that it was foreign and there might be garlic or oil in it. Yuk. They would have preferred to eat each other.

My uncle Theo once swelled up to nearly twenty stone and his doctors advised him to slim. He did. He got quite lissom and people kept saying to him, 'There, Theo, I bet you feel much better now, don't you?', and he said he didn't, he felt bloody awful. I know this syndrome. I sometimes give up smoking and, when I do, after a while my body assumes that it must be ill since whenever I deprive it of nicotine it has always meant it's got bronchitis or morning sickness or some equally tiresome malaise, and it rebels. When my body rebels I get depressed, so it all seems rather pointless. It is indicating at the moment that it really does not care to entertain another bowl of gruel, so I think I'll pass on that one. Janet was heroic at teatime. She made tunafish sandwiches for the children, and tunafish is almost her favourite thing in the world. Not one morsel passed her lips.

I'm going to bed because I simply cannot fancy a warm chicken milk-shake.

Slugging it out

What a bitter, sullen summer – or perhaps it's just me. I'm feeling very resentful because I've hardly set foot out of doors for fear of being soaked to the skin by the rain which sweeps over the hills, or blown off my feet by the wind which roars up the valley, and in spite of this incarceration I have been bitten by some sneaking mosquito which has entered the house. While there is no danger of malaria or dengue fever, being covered in large itchy red bumps reduces one's delight in living. I don't greatly care for D. H. Lawrence whose style strikes me as overheated and ooh-ever-so, but he did write one quite satisfying hymn of hate to a mosquito and I wish I had it here. The midges too are particularly ferocious this year and if one ventures out of doors after dusk one returns patterned with red spots like a Laura Ashley print. Being unable to take vengeance on the minute creatures is frustrating and puts people in a vile temper. May bugs are fairly easy to dispose of as they are large and lacking in cunning – you can shoot them with air rifles, and my brother-in-law's dog jumps up and bites their heads off – but apart from bumping into people and making a noise I don't think they do much harm, so it seems unfair. The rain has driven all the furred and feathered wildlife down holes or up trees, so one has the impression that the valley is inhabited solely by malicious insects and a few unhappy people who have been attacked by them. Alfie tells me it could have been worse, because when he was here there was a colony of wasps living in the wall, so he squirted them with some poisonous substance. Then when they showed signs of reviving he squirted them again and they all dropped dead. Alfie is not a good person to cross.

We once had a plague of slugs in London. As soon as the human beings left the kitchen the slugs took over. Avid for water, they swarmed all over the sink and, if you came down for a drink in the middle of the night, there they all were looking faintly embarrassed as you turned on the light. There was an American staying with us at the time who had a theory that you should put salt on them, so she did and I'll swear we heard them scream.

It was quite horrible, and also useless, as the next night, undeterred, there were just as many slugs slithering over the draining board. Then Someone who is the brains of the family put his mind to the problem. They could not be gaining entry through the door because it was tightly locked, nor through the window for the same reason. Someone bent down and looked under the sink, and there was an airbrick covered with tell-tale silver trails. Clearly there was a passage leading to it from the back yard, so we poked some slug pellets through the holes and the slimy slugs never came back again. I don't know why I didn't think of that. I rang the Council and they said they didn't deal with slugs – fleas yes, slugs no. I fell into despair and assumed there must be some supernatural reason for the infestation. One should *always* remember to look under the sink. We still have a few snails in the garden, but they look quite attractive as long as they stay in their shells, and anyway knowing what I know about their private lives I am reluctant to destroy them. They shoot arrows into each other when they fall in love; it takes them absolutely hours to mate and it leaves them totally exhausted, and they're all the same sex. You can see it must be tiring. I am indebted to the wireless for this information – to a programme which I occasionally hear in the morning while eating a late breakfast and I usually have to leave it. Did *you* know that vultures have constant diarrhoea in order to keep their legs warm? I sometimes wonder if the broadcaster makes it up as he goes along.

Dave, the ecologist, is another mine of fascinating information. We have aphids on our roses and he tells me that the summer generations all consist of parthenogenetic females who give birth to live little-girl greenfly. Then in the autumn the males mate with the females who go on to lay eggs which lie dormant through the winter and then hatch into more females. I think I must have missed something there, because where do the males come from? It is very puzzling. I find it extraordinary that the Creator should have bothered to endow something so small with such a convoluted sex life. And who needs them anyway?

Rainy-day blues

This is getting beyond a joke. I am plunged in the depths of Siberian melancholy and so is everyone else. My friend Caroline and I have long sad telephone conversations about the difficulty of keeping a young person entertained in the hols in the rain and the likelihood of nuclear war. I have the additional problem of getting the clothes dry, since even when I haven't washed them they are soaked by the relentless downpours. Nor can I use the airing cupboard, as Cadders has sequestered it. He eases it open with his massive paw and makes himself comfortable on the blankets. We have attempted to discourage him, but short of putting a padlock on the door there is little we can do. He is determined and crafty and must be the best-aired cat in the world.

Between the weather and the news — I just listened to it and it isn't good — life is something of a burden at the moment. A number of delightful people have been to stay and kindly helped to amuse the daughter by playing dirty-word scrabble with her, but I can't help feeling they don't come all the way to the country in order to do that, so I feel guilty as well as demented. I can't wash their sheets either because they have to be dried indoors, and this causes the place to resemble a boy-scout encampment and depresses us further. My grandfather shot himself. I wonder if it was raining at the time.

I have decided, in any event, not to watch television until things start looking up. I have seen an imaginative reconstruction of the after-effects of a nuclear strike, and it rather resembled the present scene here — untidiness, discomfort and general despondency — and I have watched on the news programmes such evidence of man's inhumanity to man and anything else that moves that I feel inclined to lay claim to descent from the sort of apes who didn't turn into us. Nor is the wireless particularly cheerful at the moment. It brings news of a coach crash, a plane crash, a bombing, several people lost at sea, a gale warning and three traffic jams. I think I'll let the batteries run out.

The only thing that has made me laugh recently is

a picture in the paper of some 'fashionable designs for women deacons'. A thin girl with an irritating hair-style and an ineffably silly smirk is shown posed with her hands clasped religiously beneath her bosom and a dog-collar round her neck. In one full-length portrait she wears a long frock, an even more maddening expression and a rope round her waist, and in another she is clad in an 'Old English surplice' with 'angel-wing' sleeves. She is clutching what I take to be a hymn book and has her mouth open. The C of E is frequently quite funny and I find myself wondering, in view of his rather negligent attitude towards females, what the founder of this institution would have made of the present developments. I somehow don't think *he* would have been amused.

I am becoming obsessed with the subject of clothes. The Aga is constantly draped with socks and frocks, and shirts and skirts, and knickers. And steam, fragrant with detergent powder, rises to the rafters. The other things I mustn't watch on telly are the soap ads, as they always irritate me, and at the moment I believe I should go berserk if I had to listen to some lady wondering at the degree of the whiteness of her whites. I don't care if my whites are white or a rich grey. I just want them *dry*. Part of the trouble arises from the daughter's habit of changing clothes about seven times a day according to

which persona she has chosen to adopt. If she's being
a Mother we have baby doll clothes to contend with as
well, and if she's being a Lady from the Olden Days she
wears mine. Having nothing else to do, I fall to speculating
on why it is that children live so much in fantasy, and
I have come to the conclusion that it is because they
are not permitted to do anything else. They have no
power except for lung power which, admittedly, cannot be
lightly disregarded, and no money, or fast cars, or drink
or fags; they do not yet see the point of reading Horace
or making lace, so they pretend to be someone else, and
I'm beginning to think they're on to something since I
am getting no fun at present out of being me. It is boring
washing floors and baking potatoes; my nails are split from
raking through the coals and scouring pans, and I have just
frizzled my fringe because I ran out of matches and lit a
cigarette with a length of newspaper flaming from the Aga
fire door. I think I'll be Katharine Hepburn for a while,
since I'm wearing trousers and a man's shirt, and then this
evening if I don't feel in a better mood I'm going to revert
to type and be Countess Bathory.

Fire and water

The sky may not be blue but the air is quite a pretty shade. We are having a new stove installed, which involves much banging out of stone work, so there is dust on everything inside and rain on everything outside. The third son has contrived somehow to break two crutches in two days and, if you're wondering why the crutches, they are necessary because three days ago he broke a toe and now can do nothing but lie on the sofa and be ministered to. Broken feet are something of a motif at the moment. Lovely Mavis Nicholson came to lunch on Sunday on crutches, having simply gone into her garden to inhale the rain-scented air, slipped on a rain-soaked stone and comprehensively damaged herself. We met again at a garden party a couple of days ago and were pleased to note from the emblazoned sashes worn by the lady helpers that it was in aid of the local bone hospital to which we all, at present, owe so much. Alfie was here a few weeks ago with his little niece and she fell over and broke her elbow. The incomparable Alan from the shop drove his motor car backwards up the stony tracks and through the streams to rescue her and sped her off to the aforementioned bone hospital. Apparently it's the best in Europe, but that's no reason for everyone to keep falling over. What was that frightful joke about the Scotchman who found a bit of sticking plaster and stabbed himself so that it wouldn't be wasted?

I am getting almost fond of the rain. You have to admire its persistence. Even in the middle of the night when there's no one around to watch it it comes doggedly down, and by day when it isn't actually pouring it is flirting with the idea of doing so, drizzling delicately down the backs of people's collars and into the tops of their wellies. I have isolated three of its modes – spitting, pouring, and absolutely pissing down – and I'm sure if I studied it closely I would discern more. The drain has started going 'aaargh' in a throttled sort of way and this is also due to the rain. Which is perverse, since you'd expect drains to be cleared by water, not overwhelmed by it. Janet made such an amazingly convoluted attempt to look on the bright side the other day it's a wonder she didn't break her neck. When it rains too much the gadget up the mountain which initially receives our water gets choked up with peat and moss and fronds of bracken and drowned sheep, so the water doesn't get as far as the taps. This is good, said Janet, because then it can't get into the drains either. I saw what she meant after a moment's intense concentration.

Quite miraculously the rain held off for the bone hospital garden party which was visited by the only sunshine we have had (except for a few of what are known as 'fugitive shafts') for weeks. I didn't think it was very nice sun – it was aggressively bright and uncompromising, and caused horrid, hard-edged shadows – but at least it made a change. I seem to be impossible to please, but I've never much cared for August. Either it has a glaring meretricious brassiness or it does what it's doing now, and it is comparable in nastiness only with February. The trees are uniformly, boringly, dark green, and all the kiddies whine with accidie and bemoan the fact that the hols will soon be over. We missed, by inadvertence, the Mediaeval Fayre, and passed on the Sheepdog Trials. Guilty, we muttered sullenly, driving by and grumbling at the unreasonableness of the licensing hours. Our preferred recreation at the moment is huddling round the Aga with a bottle of Scotch and an Agatha Christie apiece, and every now and then one of us will look up and remark wittily, 'Good Heavens, it's *raining*.' Tonight we are going to light a fire in the new stove and see what happens. I sort of know already what's going to happen. The bloody thing is going to smoke, because a demon lives in the chimney. We had an open fire there before and the smoke never made the feeblest attempt to get out but billowed back into the room with the hugest gusts. Maldwyn put H-pots on the chimney, and L-pots, and all-through-the-alphabet pots. He cleaned it and lined it and spoke to it and kicked it. He tried it with the windows open and the windows closed. He hung blankets over the entrance to the passage and curtains over the entrance to the stairs. He opened the door and he closed the door. No good. I can't stand the suspense thinking about it. I'm going to light it now. Of course the firewood will be wet and the chimney a bit water-logged, so that won't help, but I'm going to do it, and then if the worst comes to the worst I am going to lie on the floor at its feet and *scream*.

Creative cooking

I was wondering the other day as I gazed out of the window, watching the waters rising, why we haven't got a Minister for Rain; we always have one for drought, though short of performing a bureaucratic rain dance I can't see quite what he's supposed to do. I was also wondering what has happened to the man who during the last drought actually kept *doing* a Red Indian rain dance on television and radio. I imagine he's in hiding under an assumed name and false beard.

The farmers are fearfully cross, since the weather is militating against the grain harvest, and while I can see that it must be galling to see the stuff flattened when you've gone to all the trouble of sowing it I can't help feeling that this must offer a splendid opportunity to use up the grain mountain, which we are told is proving so expensive to keep in storage. I am familiar with the cast of mind that causes people to go on and on keeping things in storage, but I strive against the tendency myself. Even haricot beans and lentils have a limited shelf life, as do tinned goods – except of course for those perforce abandoned at the North Pole by inefficient explorers. Things both tinned and frozen must obviously keep quite well. I saw a booklet the other day entitled 'What to Do with Herbs'. I know what to do with herbs – you buy packets of every conceivable sort, use a pinch or two of each and then, after a few years, when they have attained the condition of Hoover dust, you throw them away.

Apart from herbs I try not to waste anything, and when I am here in the country with no means of transport I sometimes take the opportunity to use up all the dried things in the bottoms of jars. Soups and stews composed of pastas and pulses are actually rather good if you also happen to have left over a tin of tomatoes and some dried onion, and the sense that one is at a stroke manifesting both ingenuity and thrift is exhilarating. In London, it is all too easy to nip down to the market and buy something fresh, and even on high days and holy days the Pakistani shop remains open for trade, purveying all that the stomach could desire. I would not dream, in London, of offering a guest or even a family member lentil soup or spam curry, whereas here both are eaten with expressions of delight. I have made cheese sauce with custard powder and kedgeree with tinned pilchards. A tin of sardines with a dollop of Smash makes perfectly good fishcakes; a tin of mince combined with a tin of baked beans makes what is known *en famille* as Chilly Ole Charlie, as long as you remember to rinse the juice off the beans. Unless you do this, baked beans make *everything* taste only of baked beans and you feel you have let yourself down. One of my triumphs is a Bloody Mary comprising the liquid from a can of tomatoes and a slurp of Daddie's Sauce. Unfortunately there is no substitute for vodka, so unless you happen to have some left over ignore this last receipt. Whisky tastes weird with tomato juice, and on its own the mixture is like very nasty gazpacho, which even at its best is not, in my view, one of the world's great dishes. Everything left over, of course (apart from apple crumble) can be flung into a soup, which is to be served hot: bits of carcase, baked potato skins, a modicum of cauliflower cheese, old sausages, vichy carrots, sprouts, cabbage – you name it. This is where the lentils come into their own. They sort of cause everything to hang together rather than bobbing about in the liquid like so much flotsam. If it all still looks a touch lumpy and uncoordinated you must put it through the blender and serve it with croutons, which always make a good impression. Rather to my relief I will not, this year, feel it incumbent on myself to make damson or rowan-berry jelly since there aren't any. (There aren't any bilberries, wild raspberries, gooseberries or crab apples either, and I don't suppose there'll be any blackberries.) The family have shamefully sweet teeth and despise my homemade jams, which are deliciously tart and taste of fruit rather than sugar, so often at breakfast or teatime they make faces expressive of food-poisoning and I lose my temper.

P.S. It is still raining, and I have isolated yet another of its modes. Sometimes it drivels — more than a drizzle, but not quite a driving downpour. I am beginning to wonder who I should send out as a little emissary since, if it carries on like this, I shan't be leaving until something comes back with an olive branch between its teeth.

Animal crackers

Driving over the moors to Penmaenmawr we noted that the animals seemed even more suicidal than usual. We passed a sheep gazing speculatively down a precipice at a rushing torrent – he wasn't there when we came back, so either he'd taken the plunge or his wife had turned up in time to dissuade him. Last time we were here one of the sons watched a ram roaring across a field to remonstrate with something that had displeased him. He shot straight into the fence, doing about 70, broke his neck and dropped dead. Stupidity and rage make a fatal combination.

As we progressed slowly, many more of the creatures attempted to fling themselves under our wheels. Hardly surprising, argued Janet, in view of their circumstances –

stuck up a Welsh mountain in unremitting rain. Some of them, I reflected, would go from womb to abattoir never having known a fine day. It struck us as very sad; but then most things are striking us as rather sad these days. Passing through a water-logged meadow we encountered a heifer who clearly had either hara-kiri or sabotage on her mind. She stood in our path, eyeing us and ruminating what her course should be. We sat holding our breath until she decided she was too depressed to be bothered and ambled disconsolately off into the wet grass. As we came to a farmyard, the usual two sheep dogs came flying at us, one flinging himself at the left front wheel and the other coming round to outflank us. The farmer stood in the shelter of the midden watching impassively as Janet strove not to be a party to the brute's urge to self-destruction. Further on we came to a spot usually frequented by sheep whose mutton must be fish-'n'-chips-flavoured, since people who have bought their lunch in Bala get out of their cars here to eat it and share it with a flock who have developed a taste for cod, salt and vinegar and grease-proof paper. There were no sheep there that day, as there were no picnickers. The sheep have been forced to fall back on eating boring old grass and bilberry shoots. No wonder they're fed up. The tourists and holiday-makers we saw in the few towns we went through very much resembled the miserable beasts of the field, wandering aimlessly around, singly or in small groups, browsing on packets of crisps and chocolate bars while the rain ran down their anoraks. Janet has suggested that we should keep a rain box, on the lines of a swear box, and every time anyone mentions the word he should be forced to pay a forfeit. If we'd thought of that earlier we could now be drinking Dom Perignon on the proceeds.

Cats on the whole are not suicidal – ours are rather the reverse and take very good care of themselves, shaking their paws deliberately to indicate their displeasure at the conditions underfoot and whenever possible remaining indoors. Cats only play the fool at certain times and I do not know the rules they play by. There was the time my mother's cat shinned up a forty-foot pine and the time one of them insisted on following us into the village braving the tractor and the farm dogs, and sometimes on dark frightening nights they demand to be let out to face whatever dangers may present themselves, although this strikes me less as suicidal mania than bravado. The cat of my friend the analyst swims in the sea, but it is clear from the expression on his face that he does it only because he enjoys it. Cats, I think, are sensible beasts, given to making the best of things, and when you find what you fancy are their bones in Chinese take-aways, you can be morally certain that they were themselves taken away and did not willingly give themselves up.

The pheasants have been let out of their breeding pens in readiness for October, when people will come to shoot them, if any of them survive the traffic in the lanes. Already, small as they are, they are tired of life and scuttle along in front of the cars, not realising, or not caring, that they have wings to lift them out of danger's way and acres of fields to play in. Together with the rabbits, hedgehogs and toads they prefer to dice with death in the lane. The chickens play chicken, and even the birds of the hedgerow play a sort of Russian roulette, sitting on the road until the car is almost upon them or swooping out in front of us with inches to spare. Janet just avoided running over a squirrel the other day. He came bouncing out, full of the presently universal malaise, and seeking to put an end to it all, and Janet screeched to a halt, so that I would have gone through the windscreen had it not been for the seat belt. Would I have cared, I ask myself?

The last drop

Tomorrow we return to London and OK, yes I *am* tired
of life. The holidays have, perforce, been spent indoors
wringing out wet kiddie-wear, reading trivial books and
gawking at the telly, but even with the rain rising to
the roof tree I find the country preferable to London.
The only advantage I can see in urban life is that it is
permissible to employ an umbrella, a useful device for
keeping one's hair dry but quite out of place in a rural
setting. In the country it means either a sou'-wester, which
article of clothing I do not possess, or rat's tails. I never
fancied the plastic pixie hood or the waterproof headscarf;
so, caught in a downpour, one either puts one's coat over
one's head or stoically allows one's hair to get wet. One
cannot imagine Sir – as we call the neighbouring squire –

clad in green wellies and a Barbour jacket and carrying a
rolled umbrella, and one never sees a farmer or shepherd
clutching a brolly – they have to keep their hands free to
open gates and wield castrating irons, or whatever. Farmer's
wives and rosy-cheeked shepherdesses have their arms full
of sheaves of corn or baskets of eggs, or crooks and pails
of milk. I have a shiny black oilskin mac, which I have no
recollection of buying but have somehow acquired, and
about forty pairs of wellies, but nothing to put over my
head except for a red silk parasol with chrysanthemums
painted on it, and very silly it looks sitting under a window
that seems more like a porthole in heavy seas as the rain
lashes against it.

I had every intention of going to church last Sunday
for Harvest Festival, since we are now permitted to whip
into each other's churches without let or hindrance, and I
like the services round here, which are conducted partly in
Welsh and partly in English and are much more similar to
the old RC Mass than is the new RC Mass. As we opened
the door the heavens opened too so we closed it again.
Not, I know, in the spirit of the saints and martyrs, but
I think the dry atmosphere of the desert may be more
conducive to the achievement of sanctity, and after this
summer I'm not sure there's all that much harvest to give
thanks for. I have visions of some mouldy straws of wheat

and a bloated marrow. I have read everything in the house that I want to read – the Agatha Christies, etc, about four times each, all the nineteenth-century collections of short stories from round the world (and very depressing most of them are, being mainly about death, except for the Finnish ones which are about pioneering in the forests and lakes and are rather worse), and I don't feel inclined to start on *The Decline and Fall of the Roman Empire* or an old *Cosmopolitan* magazine which for some reason is sitting in the log basket. (Shiny magazines are worthless, since you can't light fires with them.) I hate games of every description both indoors and out, and what I really want to do is sit by the stream and throw pebbles in it. This is clearly not feasible, so I might just as well stop moaning about going back to London and start packing. At least there are plenty more books there and I suppose it's easier to get to the pub: just a short walk rather than a long drive.

I am also heartily sick of telly. Apart from a few treats – *The Hound of the Baskervilles* with Basil Rathbone, *Anna Karenina* with Basil Rathbone (and Garbo – obviously, since someone has to play the girl, but it's B. Rathbone I adore, and nothing would have induced *me* to desert him for Vronsky) – it has been all American rubbish with plastic women and tin men overturning motor cars, explosions and concussions and an overt desire on the part of the producers to instil loathing and terror in the viewer. Nor do I understand most of the plots. I saw a film last night where the villain was obviously killed and then he popped up again. I think he must have been twins, but it wasn't at all clear. Alfred and his mum watched it too. It featured a more than normally obnoxious American child, and even Alfie's mum took against him. She said, 'I wish something would 'appen to that kid, Alf.' And Alfie remarked thoughtfully, as they watched the maniac pursuing the infant through a number of deserted buildings, 'I think something's going to, Mum.'

I'm going to say one more thing about the rain and then I'll never mention it again. One day the sky turned bright blue, the sun beamed down, there were a few wandering lamb-like clouds *and it was still raining.*

When all else fails

The maxim 'When all else fails read the instructions'
is not necessarily as sensible as it seems at first sight.
For instance, with some foreign commodities (the manufacturers of which have confidently assumed that their
command of the English tongue is such that they have
no need of a professional linguist and have written the
instructions themselves) the directions are frequently so
inscrutable as to be worse than useless, or so hysterically
funny as to render the purchaser incapable of opening the
packet. Recently we have noticed a new development in
the style and content of what are known variously round
here as the 'destructions' or 'resurrections' – some of them
are simply terrifying. On opening the leaflet accompanying

your latest acquisition you find you seem to have bought yourself a time-bomb.

For instance a neighbour who left the district gave us his new step-ladder, as it must be fifteen years in this house since whoever it was borrowed the last one. None of us is tall, so we have teetered precariously on wobbly chairs and spavined stools to reach light bulbs, flower vases, books and all manner of things that are just out of reach. When we had to hang wallpaper we had to borrow Janet's step-ladder. Clearly we stood in need of one of our own, a light, compact, durable metal one, designed for long life – its *and* ours – safety and stability. But when it arrived it was so festooned in solemn warnings, intended to anticipate every conceivable misuse and perversion that human ingenuity could devise, that we have left it in the laundry and if we need to leave the ground we clamber on a wobbly chair or a spavined stool. 'Never,' it concludes in positively Calvinistic tones, after all the strictures about opening it fully, wet floors, wiping its treads, replacing its rubber boots, etc, 'permit two people on the step-ladder at the same time.' Now you can't imagine two sane people wanting to be on a step-ladder at the same time, so this is the counter-productive type of advice that leads people to wonder what arcane delights they have been missing out on and gets them into deep trouble. It reminds me of those extraordinary Public Information announcements that occur on the wireless – Never-stand-in-the-rain-butt-when-using-your-electric-lawn-mower type of thing.

But even the ladder seems fairly harmless when compared with our new stove. I was worried that it would smoke, but it doesn't, because I'm much too frightened to light it. It looks impressive enough – a little black cast-iron job just like every other cast-iron stove that ever was – but do not be deceived. Read the instructions. 'Do not instal this stove,' they advise, 'without first consulting a surveyor, fire officer or insurance agent.' Should you be sufficiently foolhardy to go ahead and put the thing in, they advise: 'When the appliance is in position consult a surveyor, fire officer or insurance agent.' They tell you how to open it, close it, riddle it, empty it. The instructions are so complicated they might be trying to tell you how to fly the damn thing rather than just get it to burn. It is Extremely Dangerous, they say, to use the wrong fuel, or neglect to clean the chimney, or leave its doors open, or empty the ash-can the wrong way. You are taking your life in your hands, they imply, if you are so ill-advised as to use your own initiative on how the thing should function. You must frequently sock it on the flue to hear if it goes clunk or ping. One of these sounds is Extremely Dangerous, but I can't remember which. It *must* stand

18 inches from the wall, the chimney *must* be lined, the pipes must *not* turn widdershins, all furniture *must* be kept at a minimum of 38 inches from its terrible presence or everything will get Extremely Dangerous. It began to remind me of the Ark of the Covenant. The final twist is that when you come to wash its surface (if you dare) you must use a natural sponge. I don't wash my own surface with a natural sponge. Sponges are too expensive.

In the end I rang the manufacturers to enquire why, if the thing was so hazardous, it was permitted at large, and they more or less laughed merrily and said I could ignore all that. It was intended to protect the company in the event of mishap in America where they build their houses of straw and sue anything in sight. At one time, the gentleman to whom I was speaking told me, he had worked in America for a firm that made ovens with doors that came down instead of sideways and one day some person stood on the door to reach something above the oven (he was probably too scared by the instructions to use the step-ladder), and it fell off, and so did he, and he broke his leg or his neck or his back or something and sued the company and *won*. I was fairly reassured by this, but I still yearn after the beautiful simplicity of the old instructions on the jam jar lid: 'Pierce with a pin and push off.'

Cooking the books

As I happen to be connected with publishing and the World of Books I am sometimes approached by people with manuscripts and I have come to realise that, just as every human being believes he has a novel in him, so every uxorious husband believes his wife has a cookery book in her. Slurping back her horrible old fish pie he says, 'Darling, you must commit this receipt to paper for the benefit of a waiting world and a grateful posterity' and, instead of telling him to shut up and chew his fish bones, she does. She writes down a list of everything she has prepared in the past week or so – Salade Niçoise slightly altered and insolently renamed Salade Jennifer, or Priscilla, or whatever the lady's name chances to be, beef stew, bean omelette and ratatouille and she imagines she has a cookery book. She has not. She dashes down an introduction informing us that 'real food tastes good' or that 'fresh vegetables are better than frozen', and goes on to instruct us how to suck eggs. Her husband writes an accompanying letter saying that while Priscilla was exploring Borneo he used some of her recipes to entertain the Archdeacon and now has a reputation as a gourmet cook; the few remaining xeroxes are being snapped up almost as fast as they can be copied; with a few 'decorative illustrations' it would make the perfect Christmas present – indeed a best-seller.

Some people lead very sheltered lives. Do they not realise how many cookery books there are on the market already? There are *millions* of the things: Indian, Chinese, soulfood, vegetarian; thousands of French, slimming ones, nutty ones, Olde Englishe reprinted ones – Olde Englishe original ones indeed – Balinese, Swedish, fish ones, bacon ones: absolutely all sorts. Now I have to confess that I have myself written two cookery books. One about baby food which nearly drove me mad because as soon as I consulted one expert about, say, the advisability of giving babies peach juice another expert would bounce up holding a precisely opposite view. I found it almost impossible to gauge how much basic information the gentle reader would require and was frequently tempted to address her in the following terms, 'Just use your nous, you silly cow.' I grew to hate the gentle reader. The other book was more fun. My dear Caroline and I compiled a collection of cheating recipes many of which were contributed by the highest in the land, both the good and the great, and it was received by some with breathless gratitude and by others with speechless horror. People who roll their own pasta do not approve of short cuts, whereas people who have just whizzed in from the office by way of the supermarket are very fond of them. One critic, I remember, was positively hypnotically appalled by our *Soupe Mauvaise Femme*, a cheeky little dish comprising Smash, tinned carrots and dried onions. He kept writing about it in hushed tones. An eminent lady novelist called us liars and poisoners, and there followed a very acerbic correspondence in the columns of a learned journal. Food is, of course, a serious matter, but not *that* serious – rather like life, I always feel.

Mr Beeton was clearly right about Mrs Beeton, who certainly did have a cookery book in her, but even she went over the top with some of her advice. For instance in her *Philosophy of Housekeeping* she says: 'As soon as The Mistress hears her husband's step, the bell should be rung for the hot dish; and should he be, as business men usually are, rather pressed for time, she should herself wait upon him, cutting his bread, buttering his toast, etc. Also give standing orders that coat, hat and umbrella shall be brushed and ready; and see that they are, by helping on the coat, handing the hat, and glancing at the umbrella.' I have spent wasted hours wondering what real purpose can be served by glancing at an umbrella. No wonder Victorian ladies were so frequently to be found in hysterics. Having stared at the umbrella, the Mistress is required to inspect the Lower Regions, the Master's room, the Spare room, the Servant's room, the Windows, the Gardens, the House Plants and the Drain, and offer advice to Cook, saying '. . . that we should much like to give her *carte blanche* in cooking details, but that if we did so and spent all the housekeeping money on eating and drinking, we should be unable to do what we have always done – give the maids good medical advice when they are ill, pay for their medicine, and give them wine if ordered by the doctor. Her only reply was, "Lor, Mum!", but a speedy change took place, and she remained a careful, faithful woman, until her marriage' – when doubtless she went straight to the dogs.

Apocalypse next

What a bloody dreadful year, and it isn't over yet – we still have three months and Christmas to get through. As disaster follows on the heel of disaster I ask myself, 'Whatever next? Apocalypse?' The Four Horsemen have certainly been getting around a lot recently. Apart from the more cosmic cataclysms, most of my friends are suffering sadness and dismay for reasons of their own. The first-born speculates that it may all be due to the imminence of Halley's comet, a notorious trouble-bringer. Last year we went to a sort of celebration of the beastly thing in a fifteenth-century vault under the Ministry of Defence, where we were told to pronounce it H*or*ley's comet – surely a minor point in view of its apparently matchless maleficence.

On the other hand I am told there is evidence to suggest that (apart from a couple of world wars) we in this country have enjoyed more than a century of unprecedented civil peace and orderliness and things are now getting back to normal. It is not so long, after all, since no one dared venture off Regent St. into the stews flanking it for fear of being instantly murdered. Someone has a book of reminiscences by the Rev. T. Mozley M.A. published in 1885, comparing England as it was then with England after the Napoleonic Wars. Everybody has gone remarkably quiet says the author, while in his younger days 'there was heard everywhere and at all times the voice of lamentation and passion, not always from the young, not always even from the poor. In towns and villages, in streets and in houses, in nurseries and in schools, and even on the road, there were heard continually screams, prolonged wailings, indignant remonstrances, and angry altercations, as if the earth were full of violence, and the hearts of fathers were set against their children, and the hearts of children against their fathers. But [he continues] these were not all children who brawled or lamented in the open air, and in the mid-day, filling the air with their grievances, and resolved, as they could not be happy themselves, none else should be.' Now what was all that about? I find it entirely fascinating that this phlegmatic, supposedly inhibited people, stiff-upper-lipped and keeping themselves to themselves were, only a hundred and fifty years ago, yelling their heads off in public places. The Rev. T. Mozley couldn't figure it out either but left it to 'almost any octogenarian to say whether it be not a true account of England as it was sixty or seventy years ago.'

Mind you, when I was at art school in Liverpool it was pretty noisy. The Irish women known as 'Mary Ellens' were not averse to making their opinions known, and one cry, emanating from the alley behind Canning Street, still rings in my ears, 'Lemme go and I'll give you your pound back.' But then it has been said, and I agree, that Liverpool is the least English of all cities in this green and pleasant land. In those days, depending on the weather, we would sometimes dash out to intervene and usually came to no harm.

Only ten years ago, doing the shopping in Camden Town, I bumped into a stall-holder brandishing a chicken-gutting knife in hot pursuit of a man who had caused offence. I said, 'I wouldn't do that, if I were you: you might hurt him,' and he stopped and returned, muttering, to his stall. Would it were always so simple. Both the eldest son and our neighbour Gwynne have recently felt it necessary to interfere on finding a man kicking a woman lying on the ground. Luckily the men were much too drunk to do anything more than put the boot in their lady-friends, but I don't think I should have been so bold as to tick them off. Not any more. Besides, it seems a bit pointless. Gwynne told a policeman about the unfortunate scene in which he had been involved, and the policeman said he would willingly go and remonstrate with the beater-up but there was really very little point because the minute he turned his back the beater-up would be at it again – probably freshly inflamed by the interference in his private life.

Janet was standing outside the house the other afternoon while a well-dressed young couple chatted in what seemed like amity beside the pillar box across the road. Suddenly the boy swiped the girl twice round the head, knocking her into the gutter. Then – as seems to be the present mode – he took a running jump at her and kicked her in the ribs. Janet was so amazed she just stood there gawking, rather waiting for the credits to roll, the music to swell and the scene to diminish to a dot before disappearing. Perhaps it isn't the comet. Perhaps it's television.

P.S. I have just remembered that some idiots have, or are planning to, shoot a missile through the comet's tail. This does seem to me ill-advised. Why irritate it further?

Serpentine

'I will put enmities between thee and the woman, and thy seed and her seed: she shall crush thy head, and thou shalt lie in wait for her heel.' Thus the Lord to the serpent after the initial contretemps in the Garden of Eden. I remembered these words the other day when a seed – the fifth son – purchased a boa constrictor as a seventeenth-birthday present for himself. I am not actually phobic about snakes, but nor do I greatly care for them. It wouldn't have occurred to me to buy one as a present – I think more in terms of T shirts, underpants and im-proving works of literature – but he loves it passionately, boiling and sterilizing broken shards of earthenware for it to lurk beneath and slough off its skin against, drying broken branches in the Aga for it to cling to, and warming it inside his shirt when he thinks it might be feeling chilly. It made a determined effort to slither up his nose the other day and he said fondly that it was very affectionate. I am doubtful about this. I think that if something so small (it is only a baby, about two feet long and quite slender) entertained a wistful desire to throttle and swallow something eighty times its own size, its *modus operandi* might well *appear* like affection: ardent hugs and coilings and so on.

We are having trouble thinking of a name for it. Suggestions range from Satan and Rambo to Cuddles and Columbine. Both the son and I have a strong impression that the creature is female. The dealer said it was, but it seemed indelicate to enquire how on earth he could tell, and apparently it is very difficult to differentiate sex in serpents. It is simply that there seems to be something intensely feminine about her; her movements are controlled, her clothing neat and precisely patterned; she has a maidenly, puritanical refinement, and I am informed that her table manners are impeccable. I had to be told this as although I quite like her I drew the line at watching her having tea, which must consist of a live mouse. I'm not mad about mice either, but it does seem perfectly rotten to buy a poor old mouse in a *pet* shop and carry it home to its death. (I think I'm going to cry.)

Everyone was very reassuring about it. They said Dorcas (privately I call her Dorcas) delivered the *coup de grâce* with matchless speed and skill, striking in the time it would take to blink an eye, whipping herself round its body and swallowing it head first in the politest possible fashion. I'll take their word for it.

I have the usual parental suspicion that the son may tire of her as all his brothers and sister wearied of their hamsters, tortoises, rabbits, goldfish, etc, leaving me to look after them. That was annoying enough, but it seems that boa constrictors can live to be thirty, by which time they are fifteen feet long and have proportionately grown in girth, which would mean that in extreme old age I should have to procure for it live goats and young gazelles, and I really don't see myself doing that. I might give her to Janet as a present since Janet likes snakes and lets Dorcas wrap herself round her arm amongst the bracelets.

I find this interesting as, if Janet has a fault, it is her reaction to spiders. I don't think anything else frightens her, but every now and then there will come a terrible shriek should she have encountered a large spider; or if it is a little one she will come to me, holding herself grimly in control and saying through stiff lips, 'There – is – an – arachnid – in – the – sink.' Then I take a sheet of paper and a glass and transfer the thing to the garden. The other day, having been alerted, I set off with my usual equipment and Janet said she was afraid it was totally inadequate. She implied that I should need a sheet of metal and a bucket to cope with the present incumbent in the laundry sink. She said she could see the muscles rippling in its legs and its eyes were standing out on stalks.

It *was* rather big and Janet wasn't altogether wrong. It buckled the sheet of writing paper and my courage deserted me. I said we would have to call the eldest son, and Janet said she'd tried that before and he was frightened of them too. It seemed excessive to call Someone from his place of work; as is always the case when we really need people, the house was deserted and it looked like stalemate. No washing would be done that day. Then Simon, who is a friend of the fifth son, appeared and we informed him that he had been nominated. He was a bit reluctant but bravely took a stout magazine and manoeuvred the monster on to it, dropping it outside on the path.

Janet swore that for some time afterwards she could hear the sound of its receding footsteps. Perhaps we should have bought a spider-eating snake.

Raving loonies

There seems to be a lot of madness around at the moment. The streets of Camden Town are filled with people seeing visions, many of them flown with wine, but not all. Once upon a time we used to have au pair girls, and some of them turned out to be demented. I can see how it happens. There they are in some remote cantonment, and Mama reflects, 'Mon Dieu, Marie Claire is acting very strangely. Let us send her for a change of air to Grande Bretagne where she can look after some little English enfants.' The girl arrives and she seems a bit odd, but you rebuke yourself for exhibiting English insularity and tell yourself that the inconsistencies in her conversation are due to her imperfect grasp of the language. You have to do this for a while because you can't accuse a more or less total stranger of being insane until she has definitely proved herself to be so.

I began to worry about one girl when a simply enormous vase vanished from her room. It was bright orange, bulbous in shape and about three feet high. She helped me look for it through the course of an entire day since I couldn't leave the topic alone. How, why and where could she have put it? She seemed to be denying all knowledge of its existence while continuing to peer under beds and behind curtains. I'm still puzzled by it all. How could she have caused this most unwieldy and conspicuous object to vanish into thin air? I'm cross too, because it used to look nice in the autumn, filled with colossal chrysanthemums. Then she began to tell us in broken phrases how her father had murdered the maid. This was chilling enough, but the really worrying thing was that as she spoke a little smile of pleasure played around her lips. 'Come on, Beatrix,' we would say, 'you can't be trying to tell us that your father murdered the maid.' 'But yes,' she would respond; 'he cut her all up into little bits.' And she'd smile. I should of course have popped her on the plane then and there, but I havered until the day I saw her crossing the road talking loudly to herself, her eyes fixed in a mad glare on something intangible while the children made their own way through the articulated lorries. I rang her embassy where, fortunately, they kept a sort of welfare department who turned up, took one look at her and promptly whisked her off home for treatment. She left behind the braces off her teeth, which she had frequently assured us were remarkably expensive, and I truly intended to send them on to her, but I lost her address and I couldn't bring myself to ring the embassy again, so they're probably still around somewhere.

Then we acquired an Egyptian girl who fancied herself as a plumber. She was always trying to improve the lavatory cisterns and adding shower attachments to the bath. One day, bleeding the radiator, she unleashed all the water in the central heating system and shortly afterwards she left. The last we heard of her she was in the psychiatric wing of St George's hospital, having driven the wrong way round Hyde Park Corner insisting that that was the way they did it in Egypt and she was in the right while the other drivers were in error.

The subject of lunacy is on my mind because I'm beginning to feel a little unhinged myself and it has occurred to me to wonder whether it is living in England that drives people mad. Everyone is so singularly unhelpful. Some months ago we had a professor of perceptual psychology staying with us and round about midnight he nipped out to the car to get his pyjamas. A minute later he was back with a mad Austrian woman, who had rushed up imploring assistance. I thought at first she was merely having a panic attack, because I have friends who do that, but after a few moments it became clear that she was completely off her head. She said that everything was yellow and asked with pitiable intensity whether we understood the meaning of the *roses*. We rang the surgery and were told by the doctor on night duty that nothing would induce him to visit a foreign mad person who wasn't on the panel. Then we rang a shrink, who had nothing to suggest. In the end we rang 999 and two ambulancemen came and took her away. In the morning I rang the hospital to make sure that she was all right and they could find no trace of her. I spoke to five different departments, which denied all knowledge of her. I suppose this is only because computers have taken over from night porters, but it does give one furiously to think.

Forms of torture

I think that in a previous existence I may have been put to some degree of interrogation, because now when people ask me questions my immediate instinct is to go dead quiet or tell whoppers. Somebody will say 'I want to ask you something' and I reach for my hat; or they enquire 'What is the time?' and I shuffle shiftily. I flee from those market researchers who approach you in the street with a clipboard and a winning smile, and I regard questionnaires with the gravest suspicion. In one recent case I think this suspicion was justified. A young man turned up in the country with a huge form containing queries like 'How much do you earn?', 'How much does the head of the household earn?', 'How much time do you spend in your second residence?', 'What months of the year do you choose to do this?'. All that was lacking, I felt, was 'Where do you keep the key?' and 'Are your jools under the mattress or in the teapot on the mantelpiece?' I pictured a consortium of clean-cut, up-market burglars in steel-rimmed specs sitting before a bank of computers and saving themselves a lot of aggravation. All forms are a sort of torture – passport forms, Inland Revenue, PLR, school entry. Even if you are prepared to divulge the required information I find the mind goes blank and I cannot remember how many children I have, or their names, and certainly not their dates of birth. It is even worse if one is speaking on the telephone to the school or the doctor's receptionist. 'Date of birth?' You repeat, 'Ah yes, well. He's 17 now, so that means . . .' and you count frantically on your fingers, and gesticulate for assistance at any other members of the family who may be present, and it must all sound most fishy.

Speaking of doctors, I am reminded that they are among the worst offenders in the matter of questions. I avoid them as much as possible and if ever cornered by one I tell him lies. That is not unusual. Caroline says none of our doctors has the faintest idea how much, for instance, we drink, because when asked we roughly halve the amount and they still don't believe us because their textbooks tell them that such quantities are not consistent

with continued vitality; so while they know we are lying
they imagine we are doing it, not from guilt, but from
a sort of mad braggadoccio. Psychoanalysts, of course,
are the absolute worst. Questions such as 'When did you
last see your father?' delivered in meaningful tones are
deserving only, in my view, of a crisp 'Mind your own
business.' This attitude renders a session of analysis entirely
useless and is an expensive way of discussing the weather
and the price of parsnips.

But possibly the most painful experience of all is
the ordeal by interview. Job interviews must be horrible.
(I never had one because I never aspired to that sort of job
and got married young. 'Will you marry me?' is quite a
good question, requiring only a simple yes or no, although
the wedding ceremony is a bit of a drag: 'Wilt thou take
this man . . . ?' 'For better for worse . . . ?' Yes, yes, yes,
you think. For heaven's sake get *on* with it.) But the
interview by reporter is alarming and depressing in more
or less equal proportions. Writers, on the whole, are shy
birds, wary of publicity and preferring to roost in garrets
or huddle in garden sheds with what are known here as
their 'tripewriters'. They live in a weird little world of their
own and blink when exposed to the sunlight. (Although
there are, of course, exceptions. I have been bored to the
marrow by some authors gassing away about their 'work'.

I cannot see the point of talking about it.) I have now been interviewed on several occasions and sometimes both the interviewer and I have ended up near to tears. At the sight of a notepad or a microphone I find myself overwhelmed by a mixture of terror and a mulish peasant obstinacy. A perfectly charming journalist will ask coaxingly what books I have read and either I claim never to have read any at all or I tell lies and say I read Mills and Boon. I cannot think why under these circumstances I imagine that revealing a penchant for the works of Rosamond Lehmann or Evelyn Waugh or Richmal Crompton or E. Arnot Robertson could possibly be used against me, but I do. I usually make no secret of the fact that I am a Roman Catholic, used to belong to the Labour Party, was born in Liverpool, like scallops and watching *The Producers*, go to bed at eight o'clock, etc., but when asked directly about these matters I go as shtum as a clam and I reflect – name, rank and number. Name, rank and number. You'd think that if I *was* once put to the stake I would have learned my lesson and now be an ardent chatterer – but I'm not.

The crumpet season

There's a nip in the air. The nights are drawing in. The leaves of brown are tumbling down, although belatedly. We drove to Southampton the other day and nearly all the trees were still stubbornly green, due, I believe, to the lateness of spring and the wetness of summer, but I remember one year after a comparably wet season when everything turned golden in a mad rush in early September. I don't think anyone really understands the rules. The cats are aware of the coming of the cold. They always behave very peculiarly when the temperature is about to take a dive; their fur stares and their eyes gleam in a maddish way and Puss attempts to scale sheer walls. She makes an odd sound and hurls herself up the kitchen wall towards the light switch and then runs frenziedly down the passage like someone just realising she's left her handbag on the tube. Cadders, who is an altogether solider type of feline and much less inventive, contents himself with leaping between the feet of people as they walk, like a religious fanatic under the wheels of the Juggernaut, except that he usually gets away unscathed because everyone is too nice to walk on his toe or his tail and they crick their backs and graze their knees trying to avoid doing him harm.

I am not pleased with Cadders at present. I had to get up in the middle of the night and fling buckets of water round the garden because some other mog was trespassing on his preserves and the pair of them were making a very great noise about it. I am however consoled by the fact that the water found its mark. I flung it blindly from the path into the dug-out part of the garden and soaked one or possibly both cats – which I could not have done if I'd been watching them and they had seen me coming. As it was, although I'm sure they could hear me swearing, they sat smugly among the leaves, sneering to themselves until – splat. I do not think there is any satisfaction in the world to compare with the satisfaction of getting a yowling cat amidships with a bucket of water. I have just let Cadders in since he refused to rejoin us last night, and he is roaming the shelves hunting for cat food. If there is

a tin opened he will knock it to the floor and scrape out
the contents with his paw, which is quite clever, but he
is not as subtle as Puss who has discovered that if there
happen to be towels drying in front of the Aga she can
claw them down to sleep on, which makes her nights much
more comfortable. I consider this skill (although annoying
because it means extra washing) to be almost on a level
with tool-using. By day as winter approaches, she sleeps on
MSS under the dining-room lamp while Cadders sleeps on
mine on the side of the kitchen table.

I suppose we will soon have to turn on the central
heating as it is not only the cats who have noticed that
it is getting cooler. Another sign of the onset of winter
is that people grow reluctant to leave the kitchen and
the beneficent presence of the Aga for the refrigerated
condition of their own rooms. They bring down duvets,
blankets and sleeping bags to watch TV, which gives the
drawing-room the semblance of a doss-house and detracts
from its elegance. Other people have already turned on
their central heating. I had dinner with some psychiatrists
the other evening, and their whole house was as warm as
toast. I suppose all those years spent in training analysis
must give them a clearer grasp of the realities of life,
whereas we still obstinately and neurotically believe that
no fires should be lit before the beginning of November

and none after the end of March. In leaky, draughty old houses like ours the central heating merely takes the chill off the air anyway and costs a fortune, floating out to warm Camden Town. The fifth son has ensured that his boa-constrictor has her own arrangements. She has a heated cage and lives in some luxury, compared with the rest of us. Janet says her toad, Michael, has been sulking for months at the miserable weather and is now about to hibernate in a temper.

Still, autumn has its consolations. Even though one now has to start thinking about wearing stockings, which are a beastly nuisance, and shaking the moths out of the woollies, and preparing to avoid people who are clearly succumbing to influenza, it is pleasant to welcome back chrysanthemums, which I refuse to entertain at any other time of the year, and crumpets are wonderful. Another of my neuroses is a fixed belief that no lady at any season of the year except for late autumn should dream of offering a guest buttered crumpets.

Pot-bound

I have far too much kitchen equipment, most of it seldom used, and I am never going to buy any more, so I should like to advise the people who keep sending me catalogues of culinary items that they are wasting their time and postage. I must have about thirty casserole pots in every conceivable size and almost as many roasting pans. I am not going to buy a board to carve meat on because I've already got a chopping board which serves the purpose perfectly well, and anyway I've also got about thirty meat chargers. I have eight Victorian cast-iron pans, the largest of which I can scarcely lift when empty, never mind when full of boiling sheep's head, and Lord knows how many aluminium ones. I have two fish kettles, three preserving pans (one is three feet in diameter) and a simply enormous cauldron in which I could easily poach a small missionary if I felt so inclined. I have cake tins and patty pans and a griddle iron and colanders and steamers and a set of dariole tins like tiny buckets to make vegetable shapes. I have a prehistoric ice-cream maker worked solely by muscle power, and a nineteenth-century gadget for chopping oranges to make marmalade (it doesn't work because its blade is blunt but it is beautiful to look at). I have a wooden lemon squeezer and a tin opener with a bull's head on it, very antique. I have dozens of Asiatic Pheasant plates and lidded vegetable dishes, which I never use because I'm frightened of breaking them. We almost never break the plain white plates, which I buy from a sort of ironmongers/general store round the corner, but either ancient plates are more fragile or people go cack-handed from nerves and let them slip from their fingers, and I have many halves of plates waiting to be stuck together.

I have umpteen mixing bowls and thousands of those pâté bowls that you get from delicatessens (useful in lieu of the lidded dishes). I have salad bowls and what Janet refers to as 'portars and mestles'. I have cheese dishes and a plate for serving bread with a religious motto on it in gold. I have flowered bowls for fruit compote and a Regency wash-basin to hold fresh fruit. Then on top of all that I have several Magi-Mixes and another food processor with

so many arcane attachments that it really needs a stable
of its own. I have an electric deep-fryer which irritates us
acutely because the oil never seems to get hot enough and
you can only cook about twenty chips at a time; and I
have an electric carving knife which I usually keep quiet
about because it's vulgar, but it is a great help at party
time with twenty pounds of beef or ham to slice up. The
other really useful modern device is the salad-spinner,
which saves one from having to go into the chilly back
yard waving lettuce around in a tea-cloth, and I approve
of the little implement which claws the zest off lemons
so one doesn't need to risk grating one's knuckles. But
the only absolute essentials, the loss of which makes me
neurotic and agitated, are the potato peeler and the little
sharp knife. Many times a day the cry goes up: 'Where's
my little sharp knife?' I should really keep it on a chain
around my neck together with the potato peeler.

Possessing these articles means that all the available
space is full, and even if I longed for a thing to make
square eggs I wouldn't have room for it. Where would
I put the special dishes for sweetcorn and avocados and
melons and prawns? And what is the point of them? Do I
need a candle-shaver, or scouring pad holder in the shape
of a whale? Why would I want an egg separator? I use
my fingers to separate eggs; they are excellently adapted to

the purpose, allowing the white to trickle through while the yolk reposes on one's palm. Technology can be taken too far. And who could possibly imagine that we need a stopper to keep our unfinished bottle of champagne bubbly and stop it going flat? Chance, as they say, would be a fine thing. I've already got a potato-ricer, although it, too, is Victorian and takes the strength of ten to force the spuds through the holes. The cooks of Mrs Beeton's day must have been pretty powerful wenches. Who in the name of all that's wonderful needs a wine-decanting machine? *People* are wine-decanting machines. I don't think it would at all be a 'source of interest and admiration to my friends.' I think they'd laugh.

The only things I'm tempted to buy from catalogues are in the gardening section. They are a pair of sandals with long spikes on the sole so that you can walk round your lawn and aerate it. We don't have a lawn but they'd be awfully good for jumping up and down on people who try to sell you wine-bottle drip-catchers.

Suitable for children

A taxi-driver strolling into the garden the other day to collect a passenger looked our dwelling-place up and down and reflected aloud, 'Cor, looks like the 'Ouse of Usher, dunnit?' It does a bit. There's a lot of ivy and trails of old man's beard and piles of dead leaves outside, and inside most of the walls are what is described as 'book-lined' which can just as easily give a sinister as a scholarly impression. I can see non-bibliophiles wondering what any innocent and well-disposed person could possibly want with so many books, and they certainly do collect dust. So does the stuffed alligator which hangs in a central position in the drawing-room, contributing something of its own to the faintly Gothick ambience. But books are on my mind just now; particularly children's books.

I went round the shelves today to remind myself of precisely what we have to offer in this line and decide whether they are all too hopelessly dated, and utterly irrelevant to the modern child. I still read William books myself when too tired to watch telly or if there's nothing on but chat shows or horrible old Mickey Spillane, but I suppose today's child might find the presence of maids and cooks a touch bewildering. I don't know. Angela Brazil was already out of style when I was a child so I don't expect my daughter to find any enjoyment in the *Heroine of the Lower Fourth*, nor in the unfortunately entitled *The Queer New Girl* or *The Boy Fancier*. I have lost *Castle Blair*, and my book of Red Indian myths, but we still have *The Gentle Heritage*, the works of Mrs Molesworth and Kenneth Grahame, Grimm, Edmund Dulac's *Picture Book*, and an edition of Perrault. Then we also have Aunt Louisa's *Book of Fairy Tales*, *Told in the Gloaming*, *My Nursery Story Book*, *Blackie's Little One's Annual*, *Boys of the Bible*, *B.B.'s Fairy Book*, *Uncle Tom's Cabin*, *Robinson Crusoe*, *Robin Hood*, *Gulliver's Travels*, etc. etc. etc. No need at all, one would think, to go out and buy new books, but just as they like the terrible noises they play on their ghetto-blasters, so today's young seem to need contemporary children's books. Many of these are perfectly splendid, I'm sure, but there are exceptions.

Janet and I were enchanted to discover, when we first visited the daughter's new Convent school, that the library contained many of our own favourites. We could happily have sat down and whiled away the next few days re-reading half-forgotten volumes of poetry and adventures, and the headmistress let me borrow an Emily book by L. M. Montgomery which I had never read before. I wish we had had a look at the library in the Comprehensive school from which I whisked the daughter away, before I had entrusted her to its care. The other day doing a desultory tidy I picked up a book called *Forever* by an American lady, with the daughter's name and form number (1R) written in a childish hand on the fly-leaf. The first line read: 'Sybil Davison has a genius I.Q. and has been laid by at least six different guys.'

'She *what*?' I exclaimed aloud, my eyes starting from my head. I sat down and read further with what I think is described as mounting outrage. 'Janet,' I demanded, 'what is *this*?'

'Oh,' said Janet, 'the English teacher at the comp told her to read Judy Blume.'

So I showed Janet a few of the choicer passages and she had to sit down too. She was very cross because she had plodded round Harrods innocently asking her little charge how many of the lady's works she would like; aware that it probably wasn't literature, but blissfully oblivious of the fact that it was filthy. We are told that the author has 'now written books for young people of all ages, as well as one novel specifically for grown-ups', and I shudder to think what that must be like. *Forever* is described as a novel for *young* adults which I suppose must be meant to imply that it's dirty but not very. I find the idea that 'young adults' need this sort of stuff specifically designed for them peculiarly offensive and mad. If they must learn about sex through books – and I sometimes wonder how the human race has managed to survive, much of it having been illiterate for centuries – then there are DIY books on the subject, and there's always *Fanny Hill* which has some pretensions to literature. The characters in *Forever* are about as likeable as the ones in *Dynasty*, and their minds seem similarly never to rise above their underpants. The language barrier poses some problems too. One passage reads: 'Would I make noises like my mother? I can always tell when my parents are making love because they shut their bedroom door after they think Jamie and I are asleep.' It ends, 'Sometimes I'll hear them laughing softly and other times my mother will let out these little moans or call *Roger* . . . *Roger* . . .' Is she invoking the given name of her spouse, we speculate, or is she making suggestions? At this point outrage gives way to hysteria, especially when we note that the book is dedicated 'For Randy, as promised . . . with love.'

The works of Judy Blume are issued over here by publishing firms as apparently respectable as Gollancz and Pan.

Neighbours

It can be very difficult to love one's neighbour as oneself, although I hasten to reassure you that ours are eminently lovable, seldom given to rowdy parties and always ready with the lend of the loan of a cup of sugar. Even Robin next door who is rebuilding his entire house, brick by brick, has managed to maintain good relations with all around – no mean feat in view of the quantities of dust and rubble the operation entails. One of his workmen dropping a bit of scaffolding through our greenhouse said to me, 'Ain't no hassle, man. I'll mend it,' and I'm sure he will – eventually. Another neighbour was *mistaken* for me the other day. Somebody approached her in Marks & Spencer and asked if she was Alice Thomas Ellis. I asked her what she'd said and she'd said she wasn't. Well, of course. Stupid question.

But I do think that when the Lord was on the subject of neighbours – not coveting his ox or his ass (substitute today, I suppose, Volvo and rotary mower) or his wife or his concubine – he might have said a few words about the party wall. The party wall is the Sarajevo of everyday life, giving rise to more ill-feeling than any other single item in the world. My poor Beryl has recently been driven nearly demented by the matter of the party wall. She had, at the bottom of her garden, an old wall of London stock bricks and against it there grew a rose bush. Each morning as she drank her tea she would gaze out at this pretty sight, rejoicing in its reassuring continuity, its (comparative) antiquity. Beryl loves tradition and the past, and she utterly detests change. Picture then her consternation when one morning she observed an artisan setting about the business of demolishing this wall. Questioned, he said that he had been employed by her neighbour to take it down and take it down he would, cheerfully hacking off another brick. There followed a certain amount of argument even spilling over into litigation, but all to no avail. There is now a red brick wall at the bottom of Beryl's garden, two courses short of the height of the old wall, and the rose bush was also a victim of the hostilities. To add insult to injury, the neighbour wrote to her in the following terms: 'It [the new wall] is hundred times better than ugly dangerously collapsing rotten old wall you are so resentful to lose,' and, really putting the boot in: 'The rose bush was the most ugly I ever came across. It was a wild growth.' There's no answer to that at all. Faintly punch-drunk and bewildered, Beryl now has to peer each way before emerging from her house for fear of running into the enemy.

Animals are another rich source of trouble. My friend Patrice has three dogs who think the grass is greener on the other side of the fence, any fence. She has just moved to a new house with such stout garden palings that she thought it would need a tank to breach them, but the dogs dug underneath. She said they came back from the next-door garden wreathed as though for a bridal feast with terribly expensive-looking flowers draped over their snouts. And cats aren't much better. Janet was dreadfully embarrassed once when her cats pinched all the kebabs from the next-door neighbour's barbecue. There were the neighbours looking wildly to left and right, tongs in hand, charcoal glowing in readiness and all the kebabs stripped from their skewers. 'Good heavens,' said Janet, commiseratingly over the party wall, 'what an extraordinary thing.' And the cats lay on a secluded bit of grass contentedly washing their whiskers. It was one of those occasions when the truth is better left untold.

Then there was the occasion when Cesare, Janet's friendliest cat, climbed in through the bedroom window of the girl downstairs who unfortunately chanced to have a feline phobia. He chased her round the room and then sat down, purring, between her and the door until her boyfriend came home. Janet was profuse in her apologies, but the girl admitted that after a while as Cesare was so gentlemanly in his attentions her phobia had lessened somewhat – which gives credence to the behaviourist view of these matters. But then Janet, like us, is fortunate in her neighbours. On the eve of her wedding she was invited to take a drink with Mr Mac next door, a delightful octogenarian who always kept sherry and shortbread in the house for ladies and Guinness and whisky for the chaps. So she had a sherry and when that was gone she had some whisky, and then a Guinness to fortify her, and when they'd finished that they started on the brandy. Luckily she didn't have to drive since she hadn't got far to go, but even so getting home took a fair amount of manoeuvring, involving a bit of crawling when it came to the stairs. This illuminates another frequently unremarked aspect of neighbourliness. Careful motorists, who when far from home meticulously drink only lemonade and

Britvic, feel free to drink anything when within spitting distance of their own doorstep in the home of a hospitable neighbour and end up being poured back over the party wall.

Mr Mac, who had matched her drink for drink, was as merry as a cricket next day at the nuptials, but Janet looked very spiritual.

Seasonal gloom

The prospect of Christmas is really getting me down now. Should we stay in London or go to the country? Beef or turkey? What do men want in the way of Christmas presents? How does one stay sufficiently sober in order to remember to make the gravy? How can I dissuade the daughter from making peppermint fondants when I want the table free for chopping onions? Will I have enough bin-liners to contain the blasted wrapping paper? Will the children settle for a small, rather than a forest giant, Christmas tree? I hate Christmas trees – nasty, vulgar, Victorian, German things. I would much rather have holly and ivy and a Yule log, except that the grate is designed only for coal which I have neglected to order because the coal hole is open to the elements and Cadders and Puss, not to mention all the neighbourhood mogs, regard coal as cat litter. The smell of scorching cat pee cannot be compared with the smell of burning apple wood.

Worrying about the Christmas comestibles is clearly driving me mad. I dreamed the other night that I made a first course of pin-wheel sandwiches stuffed with cream cheese and chopped olives – something I have never done in my life. I used to be able to con the kids into believing they were having a party by making triangular rather than square sandwiches, but further than that I would not go; and nowadays they are not so easily fooled, demanding elegant fripperies like pastry boats filled with caviar or little bowls of shellfish with creamy sauces on it. I suppose it's my own fault. One year I idly suggested that it might be nice to dress for Christmas dinner and now it has become traditional. Dinner jackets and lacy gowns seem somehow to demand a formal repast, ending with stilton and port, rather than a mere faintly up-market Sunday lunch. This is all very fine and large for those standing and sitting around sipping Buck's Fizz, but the person whose lot it is to haul the joint out of the oven can get very upset when she spills boiling dripping down the skirt of her velvet frock. Besides, even at Christmas time people like staying in the kitchen rather than standing round in the drawing-room making elegant conversation. They lean

against the Aga clutching their glasses and getting wildly
in the way, making infuriating suggestions about the bread
sauce, opening their presents and dropping wrapping paper
on the newly laid dining-room table (conveniently adjacent
to the kitchen).

Another aspect of worrying about Christmas dinner
is that one forgets to worry about all the dinners which
have to be prepared in the meantime. Despairing groans
go up of 'What the hell do people eat on Wednesdays?'
and the mind goes blank. We can only think of things
like shepherd's pie and fish-fingers and lamb hot-pot.
Looking in a nineteenth edition of *The Girl's Own Annual*,
I find an article on seasonable cooking for November,
suggesting geese, hares and rabbits. No one here is too
keen on goose; hares are right out because our place in
Wales is sacred to the creatures, being the erstwhile abode
of one Melangell, their patron saint, and nothing would
persuade me to offend her. That leaves rabbits, which Janet
is sentimental about, and anyway ever since the fourth son
remarked that eating bunnies is rather on a par with eating
budgerigars I have had similar reservations. Besides, the
directions for preparing it are highly off-putting. They go
on about skinning the beast and drawing out its entrails
and end: 'I was forgetting the lungs, a soft spongy mass
between the shoulders; they are removed, and help in

making the gravy.' How, I wonder? Then it says: 'Stick a small skewer into the animal's mouth and fasten the head back on to the body . . .' No, I won't. Yuk. Joints of meat that resemble the living animal incline me even further towards vegetarianism. I will never forget the occasion when a French friend served up a whole sucking-pig. I was pregnant at the time and made an exhibition of myself by sobbing quietly throughout the entire evening. But then I used to weep over boiled eggs in those days because they'd been thwarted of the chance of turning into chickens. I've got to go shopping now and I'm going to look for a simulated joint made out of soya. No one will like it but I don't care. It will be Advent soon and I'm thinking of insisting that we observe the fast. How pleasantly simple it would be to serve up a mess of pottage each evening (delicious lentil soup) and occasional fish as a treat, because I'm not so sentimental about fish, and loads and loads of baked potatoes.

Machine-gunning

Some people are useless with children, some with horses and some with machines. I fit into the last category best and have avoided the things as much as possible for most of my life; never bothering with bicycles or typewriters or sewing machines and certainly not cars. I like very very simple wirelesses with two knobs – no more; and I have not yet mastered the gadget with the buttons that turns the TV off and on, adjusts the colour and tells you the time. The old dish-washer turned into a highly efficient dish-dirtier, coating the glasses with a tenacious grey scum that made them resemble pewter and we spent ages wearily trying to wash them by hand until we forced ourselves to pay up for a new dish-washer which worked. This is my favourite machine, although it did once develop a habit of leaving the salt on the dishes so that one got the impression that everything one drank was masquerading as Tequila. The clothes washing-machine is a staunch old number that has served us for years and seldom let us down. It has about twenty-five programmes, of which I use one and Janet only three, but I don't mind this excess since the machine has never taken offence at being thus underemployed. The only times we fall out is when I forget to turn it to 'rinse and short spin', open the door and release a Niagara of cold water all over the floor and my feet, but this is my fault and it would be unfair to rail at the machine.

The previous machine always reminded me of a bulldog because of its reluctance to relinquish its contents. Often it would refuse to open, couching against the wall with a cyclopean glare, its jaws clamped tightly shut on one's entire collection of nightdresses, towels, underwear, etc, while one pranced impotently about, clicking knobs and kicking it. We had a bulldog at the time who behaved in exactly the same fashion with balls of wool, packets of ginger biscuits and the Sunday joint, but she was mad – not rabid, just clinically insane. I used to get horribly frustrated with the machine because of the impossibility of making it realise the error of its ways. At least one could raise a yelp from the dog. I would waste time wondering how to exercise sadism on an inanimate object and now I glimpse a ray of hope. The chair of the occult, or the paranormal, or whatever it calls itself at Edinburgh University, is to occupy itself with the problem of why some machines are 'user-friendly' while others will refuse to function for certain people: not those duff 'Friday afternoon' machines which don't function at all because some tired worker forgot to put the works in, but machines which go perfectly well for some people and are stubbornly inert in the presence of others. If, I reason, they are sufficiently sentient to take a dislike to someone, then perhaps they could be made aware of the edge of a few cutting phrases.

Our last car hated Wales. It would chug along cheerfully for months, bounce down the motorway, get as far as the shop in the local village and then die. Many a time have I pushed the rotten thing down the lane in my dressing-gown, realising that the only good aspect of being the driver is that in these situations you get to be the one sitting down. No one could give any real reason for the car's aversion to that beautiful country and we concluded that it was a town car, frightened of sheep and the impenetrable night-time blackness, just like some visitors we have had. Then there was the tape-recording equipment which took against an interviewee. It would whir away contentedly until he opened his mouth, whereupon it would go dead. My friend who was running it nearly went mad with exasperation, taking it all over the house, plugging it in here and plugging it in there. No problem at all. It just didn't want to hear what this particular person had to say.

The telephone in Wales frequently refuses to work for me. I dial a number carefully and get tones of telephonic refusal. I call for someone else to do the dialling and they get through on the instant, giving me looks compounded of contempt and reproach for dragging them needlessly away from the fire. There is nothing more infuriating in the world than things which are designed – which *promise* – to make your life easier and then betray you. The central heating is notoriously treacherous in this respect, choosing to collapse on Christmas Eve and selected holidays.

If I know that I shall have to wash everything by hand, write letters or take messages in person, light fires and keep candles in readiness, then I do it with an ill grace; but at least I know where I am and can prepare myself. I shall watch developments at Edinburgh with great interest, and breathlessly await the first thesis on the innate bloody-mindedness of some malignant machines.

Well-infested

I had a restful weekend in the country in the cottage of my dear friend Richard, leaving Someone and the children with Gully and her baby, Rebecca, to look after each other – which I am assured they did – not missing me at all. It was a touch chilly down Oxon way, until the fires got going, since the cottage is subsiding and the living-room door is jammed solidly against the floor, leaving just enough room for a fairly lissom person to slither through, as though doing a vertical limbo dance. There are mice too. Lots of mice. I suspect that their gnawings have made inroads into the foundations and that they are responsible for the subsidence. Richard had to keep removing them from traps and slinging them into the woods. He can't keep a cat because of the pheasants: in the absence of his master no self-respecting cat is going to keep going on mice when there are fat foolish pheasants to be had. The bats have gone, though. The roof was mended just before the bat-protection bill went through Parliament and they all flew away. Richard was rather cross to be told this. He would have saved a lot of money replacing the tiles if he had been forbidden to do so in the interests of vespertilio.

I once spent an interesting night there in the company of a bat. I was pregnant again and disinclined to get out of bed to chase it with a towel, so I lay with the blankets over my head while it flapped about looking for the window, which stood open. It isn't true about bats' wonderful radar-like powers and how they avoid physical objects. This stupid bat kept banging into things and threatening me. I didn't get to sleep until dawn and when I finally awoke a kindly neighbour had come to see if I was all right and was sitting at my bedside regarding me. I nearly died. One doesn't expect to find non-members in one's bedroom. But of all the wildlife around Richard's cottage – and there is plenty – the mosquitoes are the worst. They live in a disused well at the bottom of his garden and they wait for me. I believe they do not bite anyone else and no other mosquitoes in the world bite me as badly as these do. It all began years ago when one got me on the ankle, which swelled to the size of a largish melon. Ever since then

I'm allergic to them and dare not visit Richard when the horrid creatures are alert. The colder weather has much to recommend it. On Saturday night there was a huge gale. I still had the window open and the dimity curtains billowed like sails. I wouldn't go out in the wind because it hurts my ears, but I like to hear it blowing hell out of the mosquitoes.

It is quite difficult to remember how many species share our planet, our houses and indeed our mattresses and eyelashes. I was disconcerted to learn that even if we do not have lice or bedbugs, we are all inhabited by little tiny things, and the fifth son's poor boa constrictor has ticks and has to be bathed in a chemical solution twice weekly. The son mixes it up in a jug which I keep especially for making Yorkshire pudding. He rinses it well afterwards, but now when I think of roast rib of beef I also think of snake ticks. The cat fleas, though, seem to have packed it in for the winter. I was just going to send for the Council since susceptible residents were getting so mad – scratching and swearing and vowing to kill the cats – when the temperature dropped and the fleas went comatose. I know they'll all wake, refreshed, in the spring, but I feel I can relax until then. They don't seem to bite me much anyway. More worrying from my point of view is the way alien and unknown cats infiltrate the drawing-room. I don't know how they get in, for the french windows on to the balcony are securely barred and the front door is seldom unlocked. We know that strange cats must visit because every now and then there is an overpowering smell of male feline and neither Cadders nor Puss is, we believe, capable of causing it – not at that strength anyway. Puss, although female, was once caught spraying, as I have said before, but the smell was not strong. A kindly correspondent wrote to tell me that this can be a sign of irritated kidneys or something, but Puss looked perfectly content and healthy, so I think all that was irritated was me. One of nature's mysteries. I digress. I do not like to think that strange mogs have secret routes into the house. They remind me of members of some Resistance Movement living stealthily in corners and dashing out when unobserved to deploy their secret weapon, and I have a positively Hunnish yearning for vengeance. It is impossible to identify the exact source of the odour and therefore impossible to eradicate it. The only consolation is that at least we have no mice. I sometimes feel that we are infested by felines as other people are infested by rodents, but cats don't eat MSS or gnaw holes in packets of flour. Richard thinks his mice are capable of removing the lid from the cheese dish and replacing it. Perhaps the cats can open french windows.

Christmas casualties

I once heard a person remark, with great feeling, 'I *hate* babies.' He didn't really hate them at all, but I knew what he meant – all the paraphernalia, the damage to property and the bits of half-chewed biscuit. I feel much the same way about Christmas. I don't hate it, but I don't like the feeling beforehand that I have forgotten to buy a present for someone who has momentarily slipped my mind and will undoubtedly give me a yacht; and afterwards I don't like standing, drunk, ankle-deep in nut shells, nibbled Charbonnel et Walker chocs – which my twelve-year-old daughter always insists on trying, only to realise afresh that she prefers Galaxy – and the skin and bones of fowl. Capons this year, because I never wish to set eyes on another turkey, although I still find it strange that one so seldom sees a living specimen, and I wouldn't mind that. As we all know, the creature has ever been a master of disguise, appearing annually as himself with all the trimmings and thereafter sneaking on to the table in ragouts, curries, sandwiches, soup, and latterly even in oriental guise – stir-fried with beanshoots; but recently he has been appearing year round in loaf form, or diminished to a tiny boneless 'roast', or as burgers and escalops and sausages and rissoles. You can buy smoked turkey, or its breast in breadcrumbs or its amputated legs, and while I admire the enterprise behind all this and we have tried most of these things once, no one in the family greatly cares for the taste of the bird and we won't be eating any more. The capons were excellent and fell off the bone by themselves because we kept having just one more glass before sitting down. They were mostly eaten too, so we weren't condemned to a week of chicken pie.

Having been brought up in the war I tend to plan meals round one single left-over sprout, and have always considered wastefulness sinful. Discussing the matter once with a seminarian I was surprised to find that we were in disagreement. He said that nothing edible was ever discarded in the seminary, and I said I found that most commendable. As I spoke, a very bitter expression crossed his face, and he enquired whether I had ever tried quiche soup. This shed a new light on the subject and I have slightly revised my opinions, although I still cannot bring myself to put bread in the dustbin, and give it to the birds if it has gone green, hoping that it will indeed be the birds who benefit and not the rats who live in the nearby market. When we did sit down the occasion was marred for me by the sight of one of the dining chairs slumped disconsolately in a corner like an early casualty. I am sometimes accused of making woundingly sexist remarks, but I do maintain that no woman would do to that chair what a man has done: viz. plant her bottom on the seat, brace her feet against the floor, her back against the chair back and *push* – result, matchwood. I rather wished the man had gone round and treated each chair similarly, for there is something peculiarly infuriating about an incomplete set. And of course as I am the one who makes the gravy at the very last moment I was the one who got to sit on the stool.

There were a few other casualties over the festive season. The fifth son returning from his school skiing trip and sitting in the tube heard a Christmas present break in his suitcase. Putting in his hand to verify, he cut his finger. Happily it was probably disinfected by the rum, and anyway it bled so copiously that (I am told) the grooves in the floor of the compartment brimmed over. A fellow traveller – and may God bless him for one of those people who do not stroll past as others are murdered in full daylight – gave him a dashing, maroon-patterned band to staunch the flow, and as the boy stepped into the house we welcomed him briefly, turned him round and headed for the hospital. After three hours in the Casualty ward I wondered aloud whether stitches were really necessary and a Scotchman on my left who was waiting for an injured friend volunteered his opinion. Yesh, it was a nasty wound and probably should be stitched, but on the other hand (we laughed) a scar on the top of the finger could not be said to be hideously disfiguring; it would doubtless heal by itself and he did not think the feeling would be impaired – so we went home.

A few days later this same son, finger indeed healing nicely, went to a party only to ring later from the Casualty ward. It was not serious, he said. His friend had had a bit of an accident and he would tell us all about it when he got home. It seems that this friend had drunk enough and had lain down on the floor to rest, whereupon someone dancing had trodden on his throat and he had died. Fortunately the son had recently been dealing with this very eventuality in biology and knew what to do. He applied mouth-to-mouth resuscitation and heart massage and arranged his friend in the recovery position until the ambulance arrived. The boy is now quite well except for a sore throat and a bruised chest resulting from the massage. I don't know about the young: I don't know whether to faint at the things they do or rejoice that they sometimes seem able to cope.

On the whole I think I'm glad Christmas is over. I have reached the age where I like Mondays when everyone goes about his business and we can restore the house to some sort of order, and tomorrow I'm off to the country. Perhaps someone will give me a pheasant. Jeff gave me one which he had assassinated himself but we have eaten it. I wonder why no one has tried to breed them to turkey size? He gave me two woodcock as well and we had them for breakfast on Boxing Day. They were delicious. I wonder if woodcock could ever be bred to turkey size.

ABOUT THE AUTHOR

Alice Thomas Ellis is one of England's most widely admired writers. Her fiction includes *The Sin Eater* (1977), which received a Welsh Arts Council Award for a "book of exceptional merit"; *The 27th Kingdom* (1982), which was nominated for a Booker Prize; and *The Inn at the Edge of the World* (1990), which won the 1991 Writers' Guild Award for Best Fiction. Her most recent novel is *Fairy Tale* (1996).

Apart from her four volumes of "Home Life" columns, which were originally written for *The Spectator* between 1986 and 1989, her non-fiction includes a collection of essays entitled *Cat Among the Pigeons* (1994), and *A Welsh Childhood* (1990), her rich and humorous account of growing up in Wales. *A Welsh Childhood* was issued in A COMMON READER EDITION in 1996.

Alice Thomas Ellis has five children and lives in London and Wales.